# ANIMATION ART

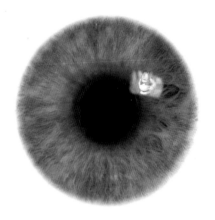

### Publisher's Note

The quality of the images in *Animation Art* varies considerably, with some, particularly in the early part of the book being quite poor. This is largely due to the availability of suitable illustrations, as many of the studios mentioned in the text either no longer exist or copies of the films included have not been kept. A large amount of picture research, using a wide range of sources. was undertaken in order to find images to illustrate over 100 years of animation from all round the world, resulting in the variation in image quality evident in the book.

**Publisher and Creative Director:** Nick Wells
**General Editor:** Jerry Beck
**Commissioning Editor:** Polly Willis
**Consultant Editor:** Will Ryan
**Picture Researcher:** Melinda Révész
**Designer:** Mike Spender

**Special thanks to:** Karen Fitzpatrick, Sarah Goulding, Chris Herbert, Beverley Jollands, Sara Robson, Rita Street, Helen Tovey, Claire Walker

This edition produced for
**THE BOOK PEOPLE**
Hall Wood Avenue, Haydock,
St. Helens WA11 9UL

Created and produced by
**FLAME TREE PUBLISHING**
Crabtree Hall, Crabtree Lane
Fulham, London SW6 6TY
United Kingdom
www.flametreepublishing.com

First Published 2004

04 06 08 05 03
1 3 5 7 9 10 8 6 4 2

Flame Tree is part of The Foundry Creative Media Company Limited

© 2004 Flame Tree Publishing

The CIP record for this book is available from the British Library.

Printed in Spain

ISBN 1 84451 234 7

# ANIMATION ART

# FROM PENCIL TO PIXEL, THE HISTORY OF CARTOON, ANIME & CGI

General Editor: Jerry Beck

Forewords: Jeffrey Katzenberg & Bill Plympton

Authors:

Ryan Ball, Jerry Beck, Rick DeMott, Harvey Deneroff, David Gerstein, Frank Gladstone,
Tom Knott, Andrew Leal, George Maestri, Michael Mallory, Mark Mayerson, Harry McCracken,
Dewey McGuire, Jan Nagel, Fred Patten, Ray Pointer, Pat Raine Webb, Chris Robinson,
Will Ryan, Keith Scott, Adam Snyder, Graham Webb

TED SMART

# CONTENTS

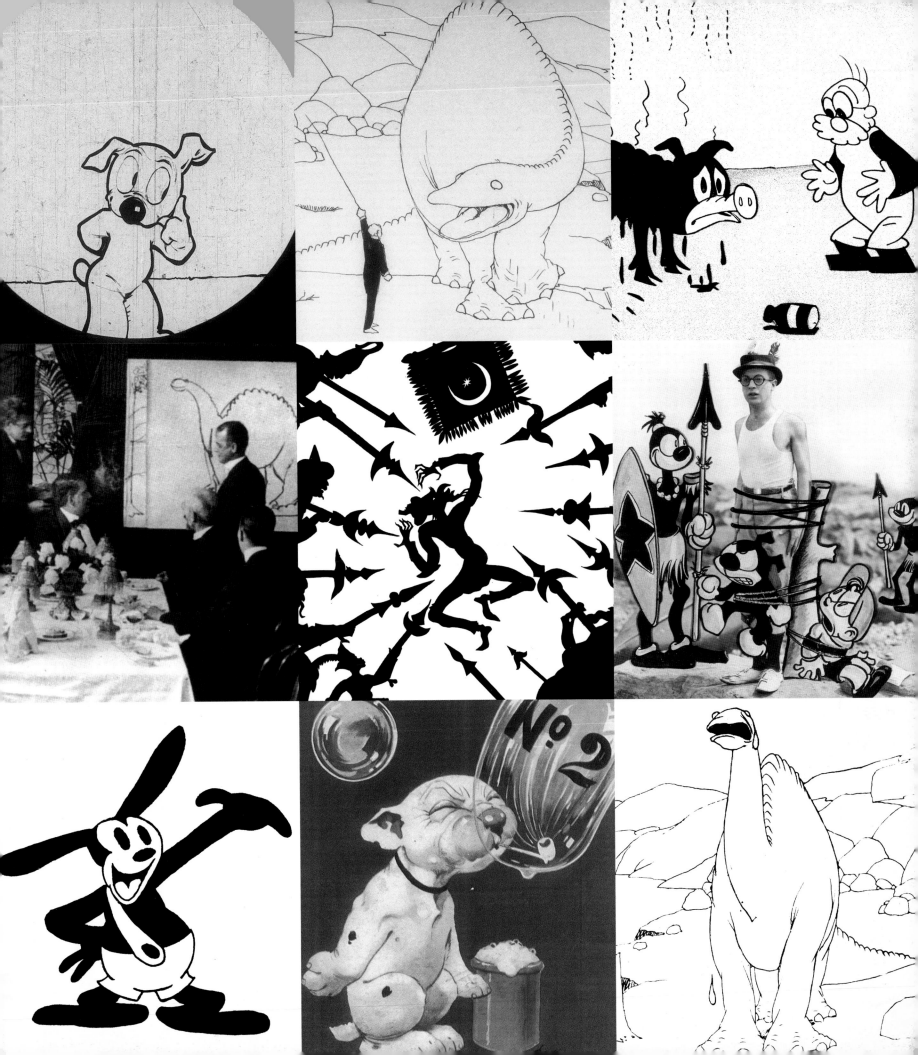

# THE FATHER OF ANIMATION

"The Father of Animation" is an impressive title. But is there such an individual? And if so, who might that person be?

### The Contenders

Ask the man on the street and you are likely to hear the name Walt Disney (1901–66); an important figure in animation history to be sure, but decidedly a late-comer to the game. The more learned may reasonably suggest Emile Reynaud (1844–1918), creator of the *Théâtre Optique*, or, stretching the definition of animation a little, Georges Méliès (1861–1933). Although none of the surviving prints of Méliès' many special-effects "trickfilms" feature what we now think of as film animation (i.e. frame-by-frame hand drawings), we certainly see him "animating" many surprising objects in the movies that have survived. As early as 1900, in his film *Le Livre Magique* ('The Magic Book'), we witness the magician/artist/film-maker transform his lightning sketches into living people.

One could point toward pioneer narrative film-maker Edwin S. Porter and his use of stop-motion dolls in his short, *The 'Teddy' Bears* (1907). A stronger argument has been made for the nomination of Emile Cohl (1857-1938). Cohl's work with stop-motion puppets and animated objects, special effects, comic strips makes him a true film pioneer and visionary. But Cohl's greatest contribution was that of being the first to make an animated film using drawings on paper. His breakthrough *Fantasmagorie* (1908), and the first cartoon series, *The Newlyweds* (1913) established his reputation as one of the medium's true parents.

If we confine our search to film, however, we may also consider Leon Gaumont (1864-1946), who was awarded a French patent for stop-motion animation (stopping and starting the camera while a change is made in the scene being filmed) in 1900. Or, again leaving aside strict definitions of the term "animation", what of the ancient art of puppetry? And, going back even further in time, some would claim that the first "animated" art appeared on the walls of prehistoric caves. To them, the anonymous painter of *Nude Bison Descending a Staircase* or some such primitive masterpiece that delineated motion would properly hold the title of "The Father (or Mother) of Animation".

### J. Stuart Blackton

One name, J. Stuart Blackton (1875–1941), has frequently been mentioned when nominees for the title have been discussed. James Stuart Blackton was born in England and emigrated to the United States at the age of 10. In 1894, he toured the Lyceum circuit in a vaudeville two-act with Alfred E. Smith. When the act folded, he obtained work as a reporter and cartoonist for the *New York Evening World*.

**Enchanted Drawing (above and below)**

Blackton was an early pioneer of the special effect. In *Enchanted Drawing*, made for Thomas Edison in 1900, he utilized the stop-motion technique to achieve the film's "magical effects".

**Enchanted Drawing**

The artist in *Enchanted Drawing* draws lightning sketches of a face, cigars, a hat, a bottle of wine, and then appears to remove them as real objects – all possible thanks to the trickfilm technique of stop-motion first used by George Méliès and others.

**Enchanted Drawing – head**

The film is complete: a hat has been donned, wine has been drunk and a cigar has been smoked.

In 1896 Blackton interviewed Thomas Edison and landed a position as a rapid-drawing cartoonist for a series of Edison shorts, beginning with *Edison Drawn by World Artist*. Blackton and Smith soon became exhibitors and, later, producers of motion pictures, ultimately forming the American Vitagraph Company in 1900. In that same year Blackton again became the star of a cartoon-related series, appearing this time as the lead character in the live-action Happy Hooligan films based on Fred Opper's popular comic strip creation.

## Humorous Phases of Funny Faces

Blackton's 1906 film *Humorous Phases of Funny Faces* is often cited as the first animated cartoon, in that, among its many trick effects, it includes a bit of frame-by-frame drawn animation from its chalkboard characters. Blackton's *Haunted Hotel* used stop-motion animation and was a sensation in Paris upon its 1907 release.

Following the international success of Emil Cohl's animated films, Blackton produced two more animated trickfilms in 1909: *The Magic Fountain Pen* (in which he again appears as the artist) and *Princess Nicotine*, which owes much to Cohl's earlier *Les Allumettes Animees*. Increasingly busy running Vitagraph, and later Vitaphone, Blackton's final credited work on an animated production was as director of the live-action footage for Winsor McCay's 1911 film *Gertie the Dinosaur*.

*Humorous Phases of Funny Faces*

*Humorous Phases of Funny Faces* featured an artist's hand drawing the faces of a man and a woman with chalk. The faces begin to interact: the man blows cigar smoke and tips his hat. To achieve this movement, Blackton used a combination of chalk drawings and cut-outs.

To make it appear that his drawings moved, Blackton would make changes to them between the frames, resulting in a sequence in which the artist draws a face, his hand leaves the frame and the faces roll their eyes or blow cigar smoke. The hand appears again and erases the emboldened animated characters.

His many credits as a director, producer, motion picture magazine publisher, governor of the Academy of Motion Picture Arts and Sciences, and industry leader and spokesman tend to overshadow his early work as a cartoonist, vaudevillian and maker of trickfilms. One thing, however, is certain. Regardless of whether J. Stuart Blackton can be considered the one and only "Father of Animation", he is, without a doubt, one of its pioneers, and — more importantly — one of the principal architects of cinema as we have come to know it.

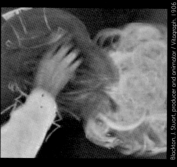

# WINSOR McCAY

It is not without good reason that the highest award bestowed by the International Animated Film Society (ASIFA-Hollywood) at their annual ceremony is named the Winsor McCay Award. Many would describe Winsor McCay (1867–1934) as simply one of the most naturally talented artists ever. He had the ability to amaze and amuse, to astound and inspire, to surprise with his skill, and to touch emotions hideously dark, joyously light and strangely indefinable. Winsor McCay was, in the words of critic W. Almont LaPeer, "the Mozart of Cartoonland".

## In the Beginning

Zenas Winsor McKay was born on 26 September in 1867, most probably in Canada. He grew up in nearby Michigan, during which time the spelling of the family name was changed. In his late teens he moved to Ypsilanti, where he attended business school while working as a portrait artist in a dime museum and taking private art lessons. But it was during his nine years in Cincinnati, Ohio, that he really established the foundation for the artistic triumphs to follow.

Here the young McCay became a locally celebrated dime museum poster and display artist, a journalist/artist/cartoonist and the creator of his first comic-strip series, *Jungle Imps*. Moving to New York City in late 1903, he pretty much took the town by storm with the imagination, skill and audacity he displayed in several successful comic strips, including his two greatest. One was the black-and-white daily *Dreams of a Rarebit Fiend* (1904) and the other was the gloriously colorful full-page Sunday creation *Little Nemo in Slumberland* (1905).

## Little Nemo

The artistic imagination, mastery of drawing, perspective and architectural design – not to mention page design and color – exhibited in the Little Nemo saga were, and still are, breathtaking, and the colorful cast of thousands remains unparalleled. Near the end of Nemo's initial newspaper run, Winsor McCay decided to use Nemo and his fanciful friends as the subjects of his first foray into the nascent field of the animated film.

**Gertie the Dinosaur – McCay & group**

At *Gertie*'s 1914 premiere in Chicago, McCay appeared alongside the screen. After explaining how animated films were created, he introduced Gertie as "the only dinosaur in captivity". He cracked his whip and the film began.

**Gertie the Dinosaur –sketch**

To produce *Gertie*, McCay drew 10,000 images onto rice paper and then mounted them on cardboard. Once they had been mounted, McCay was able to flip the drawings through a primitive machine to check his work.

Winsor McCay

Gertie the Dinosaur – sketch

*Gertie the Dinosaur* was the first animated film with a star and a storyline. McCay gave his dinosaur star a personality and emotions, by painstakingly animating tiny details, such as tears dripping and dirt particles falling.

*Little Nemo* (1911) was the first animated film to feature established newspaper comic-strip stars. In this film, a new dimension of Winsor McCay's mastery was revealed: he was an artist who had now conquered the fourth dimension, time. The film was released to theaters as a stand-alone film, but also accompanied McCay on his tour of vaudeville theaters. In either instance, the stunning animation was preceded and followed by film footage featuring not only Winsor McCay himself, but stage and screen comedian John Bunny and another impressive cartoonist (and designer and performer), George MacManus. The lasting impression *Little Nemo* (and McCay's next two films) had on audiences of the day has been verified over the decades by industry professionals who would marvel at the memory and at the effect his work had on their lives. These animated films of Winsor McCay's were not crudely moving doodles, but recognizably human or animal forms with believable weight, dimension and motion, not to mention personality and life.

## McCay's Later Films

Winsor McCay toured with his next animated opus, *How a Mosquito Operates*, during the spring and summer of 1912, while it was released to theaters outside the United States as a stand-alone film without his accompanying act. *Gertie the Dinosaur* premiered at Chicago's Palace Theater in February 1914. Winsor McCay appeared with his animated creation on stage, dressed in formal wear and brandishing a bullwhip. He was at once an artiste, an artist, a magician, an explorer and a chrononaut who had somehow captured and tamed his own impossible – but completely plausible – creation: Gertie the Trained Dinosaur. The film was a sensation, the echoes of which reverberate to this day.

While continuing as a full-time newspaper artist, maestro McCay animated other films that appeared over the years. *The Sinking of the Lusitania*, featuring experimental work in mixed media and using cels, was released in July 1918. Three films following the *Dreams of the Rarebit Fiend* theme followed in 1921: *Bug Vaudeville*, *The Pet* and *The Flying House*. Tantalizingly, fragments from several other unreleased films have survived.

Not for decades would animation dare to approach the remarkable display of talent produced by this one man, this self-financed independent film-maker, working either alone or with one or two assistants. And then it would take an entire studio of dozens of artists and assistants, under the direction of Walt Disney, to accomplish what Winsor McCay had done so many years before.

# NEW YORK STUDIOS

Although Winsor McCay explored animated cartoons as a personal artistic venture, his working methods were not practical for the demands of commercial series film production. By the time his third and most famous film, *Gertie the Dinosaur*, was finished, the first commercial cartoon studios were in place. The French-Canadian Raoul Barré (1874–1932) has the distinction of starting the first animation studio, followed by the Michigan native John R. Bray (1879–1978).

## John R. Bray

Bray was a cartoonist for the *Detroit Evening News*, and by 1901 was on the staff at the *Brooklyn Daily Eagle*. When Bray saw McCay's first animated cartoon, *Little Nemo*, he started considering the commercial possibilities of animation for movie-theater programs. Seeing the labor-intensive methods employed by McCay, Bray considered streamlining the process by printing the backgrounds on each animation drawing. The result, *The Artist's Dream* (also known as *The Dachshund and the Sausage*), was finished in 1913. Bray's success led to a six-cartoon contract with the Pathé newsreel, and Bray's first production was a parody of the 1912 travelogue *Paul J. Rainey's African Hunt*. Beginning in 1913, *Colonel Heeza Liar In Africa* launched the first animated cartoon series created for the screen. It was during this time that Bray employed celluloid overlays containing his background elements as an improvement over the printing method.

## The Bray-Hurd Process Company

In 1915, cartoonist/illustrator Earl Hurd (1880–1940) was releasing his *Earl Hurd Cartoons* and *Bobby Bumps* series through Universal. He devised a method similar to Bray's where the animation drawings would be made on individual celluloid sheets and shot overlaid with illustrated backgrounds. Hurd joined Bray, and the two united their patents to form the Bray-Hurd Process Company, which granted licenses for the use of the cel technique for the next 17 years. This development contributed to the industrialization of animated cartoons, allowing for mass production.

### Walter Lantz in J.R. Bray Animation

The scene shown here is from a *Dinky Doodle* cartoon (featuring Walter Lantz) from the 1920s in which Bray employed his overlay process. A tissue overlay would be placed on a still onto which the required number of individual cels would be drawn for the animation. The drawings would then be filmed against the background.

His first animated film was made in 1908 and lasted but a few brief moments; it was titled *Fantasmagorie*. This epic featured his puppet character Le fantôche, who was little more than a stick figure and larked about in a number of subsequent films completed for Gaumont.

In *Fantasmagorie* Cohl utilized a process of drawing the respective movements on white paper in thick black lines and then printing the results on negative film which, he decided, looked better than in positive. This white-on-black procedure was often referred to as "The Living Blackboard".

## The Eclair Studio

In 1911 Cohl forsook Gaumont to join Pathé, where he spent time directing live-action shorts, featuring the popular Gallic clown Jobard (Lucien Cazalis). He then moved to Eclipse before finally dropping anchor with the Eclair studio and, in 1912, he and his family were given the opportunity to represent the Eclair studio in New Jersey, USA. Here he breathed life into the popular George McManus comic strip *The Newlyweds*, about the problems of bringing up their troublesome baby, Snookums.

Cohl returned to France and the Eclair studios, and by 1918 had teamed up with cartoonist Benjamin Rabier to animate

a series featuring his jaunty pup character, Flambeau. He then set forth on yet another series of popular printed characters, Louis Forton's *Les Aventures des Pieds Nickelés* ('Adventures of the Leadfoot Gang'), featuring a gang of Parisian rowdies.

After World War One, the Eclair studio could not maintain their earlier status and subsequently went under, forcing Cohl to retire from film-making due to ill health. Sadly, the last year of his life was spent in hospital, suffering from burns caused by a fire in his apartment. Emile Cohl died on 20 January 1938 at the age of 81, ending an illustrious career forgotten and in poverty.

**Bewitched Matches**

The two images above are from the very end of the film and show the father throwing the matches into the fire. This film is a classic early example of the combination of animation and live-action, although then the methods for creating both were not much different from each other.

# GEORGE STUDDY & BONZO

Born in Devon, England, magazine cartoonist George Ernest Studdy (1878–1948) initially became an engineer and later a stockbroker. However, neither of these professions proved to his liking, and he finally alighted on the less stressful world of art.

## Comic Start

Turning his hand to illustrating adventure yarns intended to incite the passions of young boys, Studdy also contributed to a weekly comic known as *The Big Budget*, where he devised a number of comic strips including his best-known character at the time, Professor Helpemon (1903).

By 1914 and the outbreak of World War One, Studdy was well established as an accomplished artist in glossy magazine *The Sketch*, and around 1915 he began toying with motion-picture animation in a topical short series titled *Studdy's War Studies*. Following in the footsteps of a number of contemporary newspaper cartoonists brought to the medium of the silver screen, Studdy would provide seemingly lightning sketches (via stop-motion animation), making light of the war's more humorous aspects.

## Bonzo the Dog

His best-known character emerged from a bull terrier pup that Studdy had been drawing for *The Sketch* as part of a whimsical series of color plates involving dogs. Christened Bonzo in 1922, he soon caught the public's imagination, much like his American counterpart Felix. Merchandise embracing the mischievous canine soon followed and the market was flooded with Bonzo commodities, including books, newspaper strips, postcards, songs, commercials, posters, toys, games, dolls, salt and pepper shakers, and mugs.

To complement his popularity, producer Gordon Craig suggested a series of animated cartoon adventures be made for his company, New Era Films, under the production supervision of another British strip cartoon artist, William A. "Billy" Ward. Twenty-four hand-drawn, silent, black-and-white Bonzo cartoons were made in total and were released in Britain on a fortnightly basis between October 1924 and December 1925.

### Bonzo – the Studdy Dogs

In the early 1920s, on the back of the success of Bonzo's weekly appearance in *The Sketch*, George Studdy reused many of the magazine images to produce four Studdy Dog portfolios, each containing 15 color plates with a specially designed title page and cover, costing two shillings.

Ladislas Starewich

### The Old Lion

The puppet films made by Starewich after he moved to France, such as *The Old Lion* from 1932, were magical and surreal. He wrote or adapted the stories from folk tales and fables, designed and built the puppets, articulated every movement and shot each film frame by frame.

## Animation in the Soviet Union

Animation in the Soviet Union during the 1920s was largely marginalized, despite the involvement of people like documentarian Dziga Vertov. Vertov used animation in his *Kino Pravda* newsreel, beginning with *Soviet Toys* (1924) by Aleksandr Ivanov and Ivan Beljakov. The period also saw the beginnings of Ivan Ivanov-Vano's (1900–87) career, when he co-directed the propaganda film *China in Flames* (1925) and directed *The Adventures of Baron Münchausen* (1928), one of the first Soviet animations based on classic tales.

The most famous Soviet animation of the period was *Post Office* (1929) by painter and illustrator Mikhail Tsekhanovsky (1889–1965), based on Samuel Marshak's popular children's book, showing mail carriers from around the world. It became popular outside the Soviet Union and was even seen by Walt Disney at the behest of architect Frank Lloyd Wright.

Animated films from America and France were shown in Japan in the early 1910s and immediately excited Japanese amateur film-makers. The first Japanese animated film was produced during 1916 by Oten Shimokawa (1892–1973), a young editorial assistant at the *Tokyo Puck* humor magazine. After a failed attempt to animate by filming drawings on a chalkboard, Shimokawa drew in ink directly onto the film.

## Pioneering Shorts

His five-minute *Mukuzo Imokawa, The Concierge* was released by film producer/distributor Nikkatsu (founded in 1912) in January 1917. Shimokawa produced a handful of other five-minute shorts during the first half of 1917, but unfortunately, failing eyesight ended his career before it really began. Two more pioneering animated short films were made in 1917, *The Battle of the Monkey and the Crab* – the earliest animated adaptation of an Asiatic folk tale by Seitaro Kitayama (1889–1945) – and *Hanahekonai's New Sword* (a.k.a. *The Fine Sword*), by Jun-Ichi Kouchi (1886–1970).

Kitayama was a Nikkatsu staff artist lettering subtitles and caption cards for live-action films. His second cartoon, *Taro the Sentry: Submarine* (1918), updated the folk-tale hero Momotaro, the Peach Boy, into a juvenile modern sailor, patrolling the harbor in his toy submarine. This was the most popular of these early Japanese theatrical one-reelers, and the first shown outside Japan in Europe in 1921.

## The First Animation Studio

Also in 1921, Kitayama started Japan's first animation studio, Kitayama Eiga Seisakujo (Kitayama Movie Factory). This produced mostly educational and industrial films for the government, such as *Atmospheric Pressure and the Suction Pump* (1921). He and his studio disappeared shortly after the Great Kanto earthquake. Jun-Ichi Kouchi began as a *Tokyo Puck* cartoonist like Shimokawa. He animated a few Japanese folk tales and the first political cartoon, *The Spotlight is on Shinpei Goto* (1924). (Shinpei Goto was the minister in charge of Tokyo's reconstruction after the earthquake.) Kouchi is most often cited today as the tutor of Noburo Ofuji.

## The Second Wave of Pioneer Animators

The Great Kanto earthquake and subsequent fire that leveled Tokyo on 1 September 1923 destroyed all prints of existing Japanese animation. Kitayama and Kouchi also stopped producing shortly after this time, so 1923 is a landmark year in Japanese animation. The

**Taro the Sentry: Submarine**

*Taro the Sentry* was the first Japanese animated film to achieve worldwide success made by cartoonist Seitaro Kitayama. The newspaper cartoon strip, with its word balloons and linear story-line, gave Japanese story-tellers a structure that was readily accessible to the masses. Popular cartoonists were soon producing their own serialized newspaper prints which would eventually contribute to the development of the modern Japanese comic book or manga.

**Octopus Bones**

A pioneering cel animator, Yasuji Murata was known for his humorous films, often based on folk tale, such as *Octopus Bones* from 1927, pictured here.

**The Animal Olympics**

Designed to emulate the American animation of the time, Murata's *The Animals' Olympics* from 1928 was another pioneering early Japanese silent short.

oldest post-earthquake surviving animation dates from 1924–25: the Kitayama studio's *The Tortoise and the Hare*, based on the Aesop fable; Sanae Yamamoto's *The Mountain Where Old Women Are Left to Die*, and Hakusan Kimura's *Tasuke Shiohara* and *A Carefree Old Guy Visits the Ryugu*. Kimura was a pioneer of erotic animation. His 1929 *Cooling Off on the Boat*, a dramatization of a famous 1878 art print of a courtesan on a pleasure boat, was hot enough to get him arrested. It was not until 1927–28 that the production of theatrical animated short films increased to a half dozen or more per year.

The most prolific and influential of Japan's early animators were Sanae Yamamoto (1898–1981), Yasuji Murata (1898–1966) and Noburo Ofuji (1900–74), whose careers were just beginning in the late 1920s. Yamamoto started as an animator at the Kitayama studio, and *The Mountain Where Old Women Are Left to Die* is the oldest existing Japanese animation. The best known of his other 1920s works is *Momotaro is Japan's No. 1* (1928).

## Cel Comes to Japan

Murata, a childhood friend of Yamamoto, studied Western animation techniques and pioneered the use of cel animation in Japan. His films were spritely and humorous. They ranged from folk tales such as *Octopus Bones* (1927), *The Tale of the Lucky Teakettle*, a.k.a. *The Racoon Who Helped a Junkman* (1928) and *A Frog is a Frog* (1929), to funny animal sports comedies in the style of 1920s American animation. These included *The Animals' Olympics* (1928) and *My Baseball* (1930). He also produced art films such as *The Bat* (1930).

Ofuji produced nine films between 1926 and 1930, one as long as 38 minutes. His films were more artistic and grounded in the oriental classics, notably *The Legend of Son Goku*, the earliest animated version of the *Monkey King* (1926), and *The Whale* (1927), an art film in black outlines. Ofuji specialized in animating cut paper drawings, both fully painted and solid black silhouettes. He also experimented with sound and color. *12 Whale* was Japan's first animation designed to be shown with recorded music (Rossini's "William Tell Overture"). *Black Kitty* (1929–30 but released in January 1931) was the first with an original recorded soundtrack.

## Earliest Chinese Animation

China's first animation was created by the four Wan Brothers of Shanghai: twins Wan Lai-ming (1899–1997) and Wan Gu-chan (1899–1995), Wan Chao-chen (1906–92) and Wan Di-huan (b. 1907). Inspired in 1923 by American cartoons, the Wan brothers taught themselves animation. In 1925 a typewriter manufacturer financed short, animated theatrical commercials from them. Their first true short films, *Uproar in an Art Studio* (1926) and *A Paper Man Makes Trouble* (1930), were combined live-action/animation in the style of the Fleischers' *Out of the Inkwell* series.

## EARLY 1930s:
# FINDING ITS VOICE

The coming of talking pictures and sound on film changed the motion-picture landscape. Animated characters became movie superstars — and every Hollywood studio wanted a piece of their action.

Walt Disney led the way with cartoons that were not only funny, but had great structure, artistic merit and heart. His creative competitors kept pace with a dozen happy-go-lucky knock-offs of Mickey Mouse; Scrappy, Bosko, Bimbo, Oswald, Puddy, Pooch and Flip were among the all-singing, all-dancing league of extraordinary cartoon characters.

At the depth of worldwide depression these optimistic animated ink blots helped moviegoers forget their financial troubles. Popeye and Betty Boop emerged as favorites in this era, and music became a key component of animated film. "Who's Afraid of the Big Bad Wolf" became a hit song — as well as an anti-depression anthem.

The United States led this animation industrial revolution, but Europe and Asia were contributing important pieces to the art form. Stop-motion techniques would be refined, and new materials — including a pinscreen and woodcuts — would be adapted to animated film. The depression led certain artists, who would never have tried animated film-making, into this new medium of expression. It was the beginning of the golden age of cartoon entertainment.

Walt Disney's Mickey Mouse was not the first talking cartoon character, a title that is often awarded to him. Nor was he the first cartoon mouse, or even the first cartoon mouse named Mickey. Yet Walt Disney's Mickey Mouse indisputably made history, as did the Disney studio's post-Mickey accomplishments. The event leading to Mickey's creation was Disney's loss of Oswald the Rabbit to Charles Mintz, but events after that are a little unclear. Biographers often refer to Walt creating the mouse on the train trip home from Mintz's office, and to Walt's wife naming him Mickey instead of Mortimer. The only fact all seem to agree on is that Ub Iwerks visually designed the new star.

### History in the Making

It was a short step from design to implementation. The making of Mickey's first cartoon, *Plane Crazy* (1928), transpired quickly after Walt's return to Hollywood — particularly given Ub's record-setting production rate of 700 animation drawings per day. By 15 May, *Plane Crazy* was ready for a sneak preview at a Sunset Boulevard theater.

But a general release did not follow; nor was the second Mickey short, *The Gallopin' Gaucho* (1928), able to find distribution. Stalling Mickey's public debut was the lack of backing from a major film distributor. Paramount, Columbia and others either already had animation producers assigned to exclusive contracts, or — despite Oswald's success — were unsure about taking on an unproven Disney property.

### Steamboat Willie

What finally made the difference for Mickey was sound. Seeing the success of early live-action talkies, Disney decided to make a Mickey Mouse cartoon with synchronized sounds and music. True, the Fleischers and deForest had made sing-along cartoons several years previously, but each featured only a few scenes of fully synchronized animated action. Disney's more radical proposal was to animate an entire one-reel cartoon story, *Steamboat Willie* (1928), to a predetermined tempo.

Walt devised a several-step production plan. Scenes were timed to a predetermined tempo, then animated and filmed. Only then was the music recorded, with Walt traveling to New York for a session with band leader Carl Edouarde. Edouarde's band watched the film while playing the score — and were kept in step by a bouncing visual cue, hand-drawn by Iwerks on the film frames of a workprint.

The final step of mating music with film was handled by Pat Powers, owner of the Cinephone sound-on-disc system. Powers was also an independent movie distributor. As no big contract had as yet materialized for Mickey, Powers' Celebrity Pictures did the honors for *Willie* and the year of Disney shorts that followed.

© The Walt Disney Company

**Steamboat Willie**

Walt Disney decided that his third Mickey Mouse film, *Steamboat Willie*, would be made with sound. He and a musician from his studio, Wilfred Jackson, found a way to synchronize the sound to the film using a harmonica and a metronome. They perfected their system, and *Steamboat Willie* opened on 18 November 1928.

© The Walt Disney Company

Ub Iwerks designed Walt Disney's most recognizable character, Mickey Mouse. He drew the storyboards and the sketches used to animate the early Mickey Mouse cartoons; Walt Disney was the voice of Mickey.

© Alexandre Alexeieff / National Film Board of Canada

creation, *Night on Bald Mountain* (1933), using his own, painstaking device of animating known as the pinscreen.

## The Pinscreen Technique

The instrument used to create this type of animation can best be described as an upright white plate, perforated with tiny holes into which slide the same number of steel rods (or pins). When illuminated correctly, small rollers are used to push the pins in to the degree needed to create a satisfactory image. The solitary picture is then photographed and subsequently altered to the next position. Perfect lighting and shadow contribute to create the illusion of a finely engraved pastel etching.

Alexeieff did not touch the screen until World War Two, when he was asked to produce entertainment films for the National Film Board of Canada. The most endearing entry is *En Passant* ('In Passing', 1943), a light-hearted interpretation of Canadian folk songs. Returning to publicity films, Alexeieff continued making films with his American-born wife, Claire Parker (1906–81), and did not touch the pinscreen until his interpretation of Nikolai Gogol's grim tale of an individual obsessed by his own nose, *Le Nez* ('The Nose', 1965).

**En Passant**

*En Passant* was made using the revolutionary pinscreen technique. With this, it was possible to create a range of dramatic textural effects and shading variations from black to white, through various grays that was difficult to achieve with the more traditional medium of cel animation.

**Le Nez**

*Le Nez*, created using Alexeieff's pinscreen technique, demonstrated the etching-like results that could be achieved with this method. The thousands of pins inserted into the screen would be moved between photographing frames, enabling subtle shadow effects to be created.

© Alexandre Alexeieff

István Kiszly Kató was the father of Hungarian animation. The graphic artist and creator of weekly cartoon news bulletins made his first film in 1914 using cut-outs. He made a few short films, including *Janos the Knight* (1916) and *Romeo and Juliet* (1931), but unable to find much support for his work, he turned instead to education and advertising animation film production.

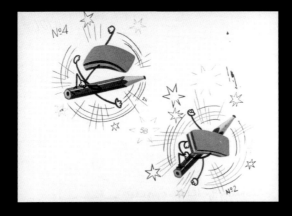

## The Beginnings

Hungarian animation, however, did not really begin until the 1930s when a former painter named Sándor Bortnyik opened up a school for the art of promotion in 1928. At this school, a young graphic artist named Gyula Macskássy met János Halász (1912–95). In 1932, the duo founded a studio that produced over 100 advertising cartoons, using a wide range of animation techniques. Unfortunately, many of Macskássy's colleagues left Hungary to pursue artistic ambitions that simply could not be realized in Hungary. Among those to emigrate were János Halász, who moved to England and changed his name to John Halas, and György Marczincsák (1908–80), who became George Pal.

A few artists, including Macskássy, continued to work on both artistic and commercial animation projects with varying degrees of success. But with a limited market for animation shorts, Hungarian animation would have to wait until the end of World War Two to find an identity and an audience.

### Pencil and Rubber – sequence

Made by Hungarian pioneer animator Gyula Macskássy in 1960, this short won the country its first prize at an international festival. The foundations of his career were laid during the 1930s when he made commercials using all kinds of diverse animation techniques, which could be seen as individual cartoons in their own right.

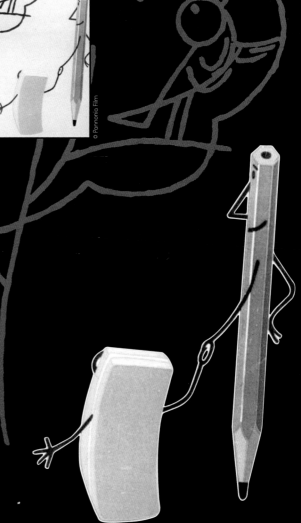

## Berthold Bartosch

Berthold Bartosch (1893–1968) was born in Polaun, Bohemia (now called Polubny and part of the Slovak Republic). At age 18, he moved to Vienna to study architecture. On the advice of one of his art teachers, Bartosch began making educational animation films. In 1919, he moved to Berlin to continue this work. While there he met many artists, including German animator Lotte Reiniger. Bartosch worked on some of Reiniger's silhouette animation films before being approached by German publisher Kurt Wolff to make a film version of an illustrated storybook by Flemish artist Frans Masereel. Wolff wanted Bartosch to re-create Masereel's wood engravings on film. Bartosch agreed, moved to Paris, and for two years, much of it in his apartment, worked on the film *L'idée* ('The Idea', 1931). It would be his only surviving work.

© Bertold Bartosch

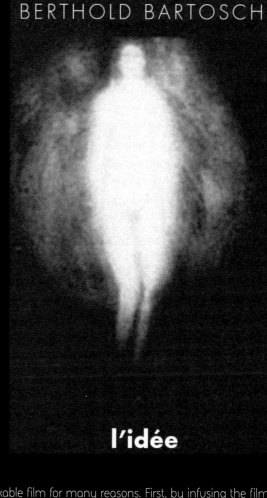

**l'idée**

### L'idée – sequence

Bartosch's *L'idée* was tragic, symbolist allegory of man's struggle for the Ideal, based on illustrations by Franz Masereel and with music by Arthur Honegger. Bartosch combined cut-out silhouettes on the lines of the Reiniger technique with subtle effects achieved by control of photographic exposure and diffusion of the light source.

### The Greedy Bee

Gyula Macskássy (later to become George Pal), who began his career in animation by founding a studio with János Halász (later to become John Halas) in the 1930s producing commercials, went on to make Hungary's first animated cartoons, such as the one pictured here from 1958.

### The Idea

The plot of *L'idée* is simple. A man conjures up his idea of beauty and purity through the figure of a young woman. While some try to manipulate, intimidate and destroy the idea, it carries on untouched and spreads throughout the world.

*L'idée* was a remarkable film for many reasons. First, by infusing the film with poetics, politics and personal expression, Bartosch shows us that animation can match any of the great art forms. Secondly, *L'idée* is a technical marvel. Bartosch animated approximately 45,000 frames on four levels of glass sheets, sometimes with as many as 18 superimpositions involved. The soft, milky, iridescent atmosphere was created using wash-tinted blacks and a normal bar of soap, which were then lit from below by 100-watt lightbulbs.

In the end, it was never released, and Bartosch never made any money from it. After his second film was destroyed during the war, Bartosch spent his last years concentrating on painting.

© Pannonia Film

The early 1930s saw Japanese animation become more closely tied to the increasingly nationalistic spirit following Japan's military incursions into Chinese Manchuria. There were still many art films and adaptations of folk tales, but it was becoming important to gain the goodwill and patronage of the government and the Imperial Navy, which considered animated films to be excellent for anti-Western domestic propaganda.

### Kenzo Masaoka

Kenzo Masaoka (1898–1988) was one of Japan's leading animators during the early period of sound films. He produced the first series of a two-film story, the cut-paper animation *A Shipwreck Tale: Part 1, Monkey Island*, and its sequel, *Part 2, The Pirate Ship* both in 1931. His 1933 cartoon animation *The World of Power and Women*, a comedy for adults, was Japan's first animated film with an optical soundtrack. The 1934 children's cartoon animation *Tahchan's Trip to the Bottom of the Sea* showed Masaoka's interest in experimenting in all production media to produce animation for all age groups.

### Yasuji Murata

Masaoka and Noburo Ofuji did not support Japan's growing nationalism and kept to folkloric, art and non-political humorous films. Yasuji Murata continued to animate folk tales such as *The Monkey's Big Catch* (1933, released January 1934), but he also produced the first propaganda cartoon, *Aerial Momotaro* (1931). This portrayal of the young folk-tale hero and his anthropomorphized animal companions as modern fighter pilots, who become peacemakers in a war between penguins and albatrosses, glamorized both the military and the concept of Japan as the benevolent "big brother" of all other Asiatic/Pacific peoples. In 1933–34 Murata directed the first animated series based on a popular Japanese comic strip, a four-film adaptation of *Norakuro* (*Black Dog*) by Shiho Tagawa, starring a dog recruit in a funny-animal army: *Buck Private Norakuro – Training, Buck Private Norakuro – Drills, Sergeant Norakuro*, and *2nd Lieutenant Norakuro – The Sunday Mystery*.

### Propaganda Animation

Mitsuyo Seo (b. 1911) started off as Masaoka's assistant, but quickly graduated to producer/director. His first films were *The Mischievous Little Ant* (1933) and *Sankichi the Monkey – Air Defense Military Exercise* (1933), the latter a militaristic funny-animal comedy. Seo would evolve from producing both general cartoons and martial cartoons

© Kenzo Masaoka

**Shipwreck Tale**

From the first part of this film story by Kenzo Masaoka, this short was made using cut-paper animation and was one of Japan's earliest animation films to use sound.

to only the latter, culminating in Japan's first wartime propaganda animated feature.

The first clearly anti-Western animation was Takao Nakano's *Black Cat Hooray!* (April 1934), in which a party of dolls in Japanese costumes and traditional Japanese toys are attacked by vicious bandits who are rat parodies of Mickey Mouse and snake parodies of American or British sailors. Momotaro and other Japanese folk heroes save the day. As the 1930s progressed, animation such as this would become more common.

Some animators created studio names for themselves, such as Murata's Yokohama Cinema Kyokai and Seo's Nihon Manga Film Kenkuyo. But their films remained essentially individual hobbyist productions, animated at home or in a small office by the animator and a few assistants. They did, however, get increasing financing from the professional motion picture companies, who paid for their production materials in return for distribution rights.

## China

After Japan effectively annexed Manchuria from China in 1931, a wave of nationalism and anti-Japanese feeling swept China. The Wan Brothers took advantage of this to produce propagandistic animation such as *The Price of Blood* (1932). In 1933 the

© Yasuji Murata

**Norakuro (Black Dog)**
This animated series, Japan's first, reflected the growing influence of the military in Japanese society. It also emphasises the stylistic shift that had been taking place during the 1930s away from folk tales towards faster-paced, Western-style humor.

Mingxing Film Company in Shanghai hired Lai-ming, Gu-chan and Chao-chen to set up an animation unit. The Wan Brothers utilized both cut-paper and cel animation for popular entertainment, as well as patriotic films such as *The Sad State of the Nation* and *Aviation Saves China*, until 1937, when the Japanese capture of Shanghai closed the studio.

The Wan Brothers and Early Chinese Animation » 31  Wan Brothers and wartime » 114

# 1934–39:
# TECHNICOLOR FANTASIES

Technicolor brought a new look to animated films of the 1930s. The depression made everything seem gray – so delightful multicolored flights of fancy created by Hollywood's screen cartoonists were welcomed and rewarded. The Hollywood Production Code cleaned up the frequent outhouse humor and Betty Boop's risqué antics – but the public was dazzled by evolving new techniques, more sophisticated storytelling and advanced visuals.

Animation art grew in exciting ways during this period. Extra-length shorts and feature-length films emerged. Multi-plane and Stereoptical backgrounds gave depth to the previously flat cartoon landscapes. Full character animation allowed greater personality development. Professional voice actors got into the game – Mel Blanc in particular – giving cartoon stars broader appeal.

Oskar Fischinger and George Pal became leading animators in Europe with their innovative work. Creativity, artistry and commercial success seemed to work together during this period. The highlight of this era, Walt Disney's *Snow White and the Seven Dwarfs*, is an incredible feature film, and influenced the shape of animation for the rest of the century. Its impact was felt worldwide, and it gave animated films a new status.

It was the period when animation came of age.

Disney's *Silly Symphonies* advanced the art of animation storytelling. These heartwarming shorts were a welcome dose of laughter for a nation in the grip of the Great Depression. Jobs were scarce across America, but the Disney studio expanded its staff in 1934–35. Referred to as "the nine old men", Les Clark, Frank Thomas, Ollie Johnston, Milt Kahl, Marc Davis, Wolfgang "Woolie" Reitherman, Eric Larson, John Lounsbery and Ward Kimball formed the core group of animators who would become the talent pool on many features to come.

## Donald Duck

In 1934 the world was introduced to a character who, starting only as a bit player in *Wise Little Hen*, would become almost as synonymous with Disney as Mickey Mouse – Donald Duck. Clarence Nash was the voice actor who brought life to the nearly unintelligible fowl. The audience's and animators' instant love for the zany character, which was chiefly developed by animator Dick Lundy, allowed him to move from *Silly Symphonies* to Mickey's gang in *Orphan's Benefit*.

### Clock Cleaners

A classic nine-minute short, *Clock Cleaners* features "the gang" – Mickey Mouse, Donald Duck and Goofy – as cleaners working in a clock tower that has a mind of its own.

## The Gang

In 1935, story department head Ted Sears formulated detailed analyses of all of the characters' personalities for the staff to use as a reference. That same year, the first color Mickey Mouse cartoon, *The Band Concert*, debuted and two *Silly Symphonies*, *The Tortoise and the Hare* – with its notable advancements in the representation of speed – and *Three Orphan Kittens*, shared the Academy Award for Best Animated Short. An explosion of creativity erupted in 1936 with the premiere of nine Mickey Mouse shorts, including *Thru the Mirror*, which transported Mickey into the *Through the Looking Glass* story, and *Moving Day*, which featured Mickey, Donald and Goofy being evicted from their home, a clear reference to a common experience of the day. By now, Donald Duck had become so popular that he was given his own starring role in *Donald and Pluto*.

In 1937, with many of the artists graduating from the shorts to work on *Snow White*, only three *Silly Symphonies* were released – *Woodland Café*, *Little*

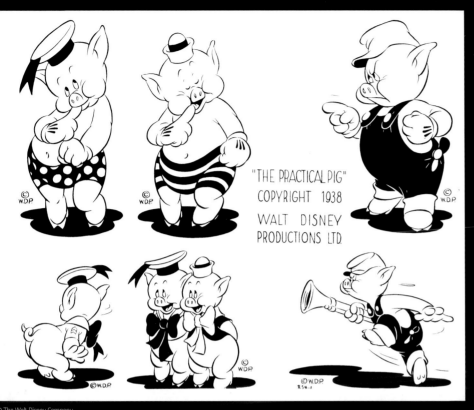

"THE PRACTICAL PIG"
COPYRIGHT 1938
WALT DISNEY
PRODUCTIONS LTD.

*Hiawatha* and *The Old Mill* – the latter marking the first use of the multi-plane camera. This breakthrough in animation utilized backgrounds painted on glass that were set at varying distances, creating an increased sense of depth. The short garnered an Oscar for Best Cartoon, as well as a technical award for developer Bill Garity and his team. This year also continued the successful pairing of Mickey, Donald and Goofy as "the gang", producing some of the most memorable shorts of all time, such as *Hawaiian Holiday*, *Clock Cleaners* and *Lonesome Ghosts*. Two more "Mickey Mouse" cartoons were released that year starring a solo Donald – *Don Donald* and *Modern Inventions*, the latter featuring the debut of Donna Duck, later renamed Daisy. Donald's next solo appearance – *Donald's Ostrich* – would mark the first short labeled as a Donald Duck cartoon. Pluto also received his first starring role in *Pluto's Quin-Puplets*.

## The Practical Pig

One of the last *Silly Symphonies* to be made, *The Practical Pig* is a sequel to the classic short *Three Little Pigs*. After this, Disney began to focus more on feature films.

## The Old Mill

Famous for being the first animation to make use of the multi-plane camera technique, pioneering *Silly Symphony*, *The Old Mill* was made in 1937. Developed by the Disney studio, the multi-plane camera gave added depth to background shots.

## Mickey's Circus – sketch

Released in 1936, *Mickey's Circus* features Mickey and Minnie Mouse and Donald Duck, shown in this graphite-on-paper animation drawing after having trouble with his sea-lion act.

## Redesigning an Icon

In an attempt to revitalize Mickey in the face of Donald Duck's ever-growing popularity, animator Fred Moore was allowed to redesign the famous mouse (shrinking his cheeks and adding whites to his eyes), which debuted in 1939's *The Pointer*. "The gang" had become so famous that Goofy was given his own series, starting with *Goofy and Wilbur*. By this time, the shorts had moved away from gags and focused more on character development, which some said made them too refined. The end of the decade stood as a major transition for Disney. That year would see the end of *Silly Symphonies* with the *Three Little Pigs* sequel, *The Practical Pig*, and the color remake of *The Ugly Duckling*, which won an Oscar. The success of *Snow White* allowed the company to move to a bigger studio in Burbank, where the studio remains today, and the focus began to shift from shorts to features.

# SNOW WHITE

By 1934, Walt Disney had realized that the success of the shorts would not sustain the studio forever. He assembled his artists and told them the story of *Snow White and the Seven Dwarfs*, which had been dear to him since his childhood. Riding the enthusiasm of Disney, the artists were ecstatic. However, many Hollywood observers thought the venture was doomed, fearing adults would not respond to a long-form animated film.

## Taking a Chance

Disney understood the daunting challenges the undertaking of the film would entail. The story was kept simple, but the original fairy tale needed to be fleshed out and pacing became essential. Disney felt an audience could not endure a short's frantic pace for 70 minutes. He also wanted the scenes to flow naturally into one another, and ultimately ordered painful cuts of whole sections that did not serve the story. Another key issue was developing distinct personalities for all seven dwarves, much like the work done on *Three Little Pigs*. The most criticized portion was the rendering of the realistic human characters, which were Rotoscoped, a process of tracing live-action actors' movements.

## A Learning Curve

For this enormous production, the studio enlisted all of its top artists, including Art Babbitt, Shamus Culhane, Hamilton Luske, Fred Moore, Norman Ferguson, Vladimir "Bill" Tytla and Myron "Grim" Natwick. The film served as a learning experience every step of the way. Long hours were spent redoing detailed scenes to get them just right. For instance, Culhane took six months to animate the one-minute "Heigh Ho" segment.

With the increased amount of dialogue, the animators found they needed to use more body language when characters spoke. Ferguson, a movement master and the chief animator behind the development of Pluto, was in charge of bringing the Queen to life and creating her terrifying transformation into the wicked witch. Natwick oversaw Snow White and found, unlike the dwarves whose cartoony looks allowed more room for error, each pose of Snow White had to be perfect or the movement would appear jumpy. Tytla, one of the studio's most respected animators, oversaw Grumpy, and along with Don Graham, was key in developing the talents of the young animators, who started on the *Silly Symphonies* and moved on to *Snow White*. Many of the studio's legendary "nine old men" started out as assistants on the project.

*© The Walt Disney Company*

**The Seven Dwarfs**

Walt Disney knew it was imperative to develop individual personalities for all seven of the dwarves in order to maintain the interest and sympathy of an audience. In order to animate the human characters realistically, the animators had to study anatomy and footage of live-action models.

*© The Walt Disney Company*

© The Walt Disney Company

## Snow White

This original painting on celluloid was used in the filming of *Snow White*. The huge success of the film meant that Disney could turn his attention to producing feature-length films as opposed to animated shorts.

## Disney Artist

Animation began in 1936, and ultimately more than 750 artists worked on *Snow White*, including 32 animators, 102 animation assistants, 20 layout men, 25 background artists, 65 effects animators, and 158 inkers and painters. In all, at least two million sketches were created and more than 250,000 drawings were used on-screen.

## Phenomenal Success

After years of arduous work, the film, which was now six times over its initial budget at almost $1.5 million, debuted in a gala Hollywood premiere on 21 December 1937. It was an instant phenomenon.

Disney, always the savvy businessman, saw an opportunity, and for the first time in history had merchandising lined up before the film was released so fans could run to the nearest department store and take home a piece of the magic. The emotional depth of the tale and subtle humanity of the animated characters awed critics and audiences. This was a film that launched an entire industry and changed cinema forever.

*Bambi* » 82  *The Lion King* » 304

# COLOR CLASSICS

Animated cartoons in the 1930s saw tremendous technical advancements: first with the introduction of sound, and next with the addition of color. Although Walt Disney's *Flowers and Trees* (1931) launched the color cartoon era, there were earlier efforts going back to the silents. The earliest known color cartoon in the United States is Bray's 1920 release, *The Debut of Thomas Cat*, made in the Brewster Color Process. Other color systems, such as Synthechrome by Carpenter-Goldman Laboratories and two-color Technicolor, continued to develop well into the 1920s. These color systems, however, used only red and green, or red and blue, which limited their range in color reproduction.

## The Technicolor Process

Ub Iwerks released his premier Flip the Frog cartoon, *Fiddlesticks*, in two-color Technicolor. But it was the introduction of the three-color Technicolor process in the early 1930s that resulted in the greatest improvement, presenting the widest possibilities for animated cartoons. Although Technicolor representatives approached the various studios, it was independent producer Walt Disney who took the gamble that paid off. This was a bold risk on the part of both Disney and Technicolor Corporation.

## Max Fleischer and Fleischer Studios

The depression in the United States was at its height in the year 1931. Disney was struggling financially, many times going through lay-off periods due to interruptions of cash flow. The largest cartoon studio at the time was Fleischer Studios, due to their ties with Paramount. Max Fleischer was immediately interested in Technicolor, but was denied the opportunity due to the corporate reorganization brought on by Paramount's first series of bankruptcies in the 1930s. Fleischer's loss became Disney's gain.

The value of color cartoons was being realized in the same respect as sound cartoons of the early talkie period. Cartoons were easier and cheaper to produce in color, adding value and prestige to the black-and-white theatrical program. By 1934, Paramount had consented to the production of a color series, *Color Classics*, to be produced by Fleischer. But with Disney's exclusivity to three-color Technicolor, Fleischer was forced to use the available two-color processes for the first two years. The series began with *Poor Cinderella* (1934), which used the red-and-blue Cinecolor process. All other releases were made in the red-and-green two-color Technicolor process until 1936. The addition of the Stereoptical process, which created a third-dimensional background effect, offered compensation for the limited color spectrum – and a feature that was unique from Disney.

But by 1936, Disney's exclusivity had expired, and Fleischer Studios released its first, and possibly best, *Color Classic*, *Somewhere in Dreamland* in the three-color Technicolor process.

**Dave Fleischer**

Dave Fleischer received director credit on every Max Fleisher cartoon. As Max's brother he began his affiliation with the studio by dressing up as a clown and being photographed and Rotoscoped for the early Koko experiments.

© Fleischer Studio

### Aladdin and His Wonderful Lamp – sketch

During the 1930s Fleischer put his biggest star in three Technicolor specials. *Popeye Meets Sindbad* (1936) and *Popeye Meets Ali Baba* (1937) contain elaborate three-dimensional settings and a lavish color palatte. *Aladdin and his Wonderful Lamp* (1939) was the final one in the series.

© Fleischer Studio/King Features

# COMPETING WITH DISNEY

Walt Disney created the market for color cartoons, and by 1934 other producers had begun to follow him. Ub Iwerks started releasing cartoons, with the *ComiColor* and *Willie Wopper* series in red-and-blue Cinecolor. At the same time, Charles Mintz started the production of the *Color Rhapsody* series for Columbia, beginning with *Holiday Land* (1934).

## A Rainbow of Color

Burt Gillett (1891–1971) revamped the Van Beuren Studio with *The Rainbow Parade*, first using two-color Technicolor and later the three-color process. *Merrie Melodies* became Warner's color cartoon series, and under their new association with MGM, Harmon and Ising started producing color *Happy Harmonies*. Walter Lantz produced six *Cartune Classic* cartoons for Universal in two-color Technicolor, then returned to black and white until 1939. Paul Terry waited until 1938 before releasing *Terrytoons* in full Technicolor. Aside from the obvious addition of color, all of these cartoons were conceived with common elements: musical, fairy tale fantasies fashioned in the "Disney" mode. And as Disney continued to move forward, the entire industry seemed poised to follow his next move, animated features.

Although his competitors referred to it as a folly, they underestimated Disney's vision and the secret to his successes. Unlike other cartoon producers, Disney was using animation as a means to achieving serious success as a cinematic storyteller. And as Disney gained more experience as a film-maker, he focused on emotional elements instead of comedy for its own sake. This effort is what separated Disney from other cartoon makers, but his drive to continually raise standards elevated costs to such an extent that his only means of financial survival would be in animated features. This was proved in Walt Disney's production of *Snow White and the Seven Dwarfs*.

## Gulliver's Travels

It has been assumed that Max Fleischer's motivation for producing *Gulliver's Travels* was to imitate Disney's success, but internal memos indicate that Fleischer had plans to make features as early as 1934, and Fleischer Studios was the only other studio large enough to undertake such a level of production. Paramount discouraged Fleischer's

**Gulliver's Travels – face**

The character of Gulliver was Rotoscoped – a method devised by the Fleischers where the drawing was achieved by tracing over the movements of a live actor.

**Gulliver's Travels – leg**

A milestone in the art of animation, *Gulliver's Travels* was the second animated motion picture of its magnitude ever produced, and the first animated feature from a studio other than Disney.

© Paramount

© Paramount

POPEYE'S FILM CREATOR, MAX FLEISCHER

PIVOT AROUND WHICH TABLE REVOLVES – PIVOT IS 6 FEET FROM LENS

WHAT THE CAMERA SEES

SET SHOWS THROUGH BEHIND CELLULOID

ANIMATED CHARACTER ON CELLULOID

CUT-OUT SILHOUETTE OF TREE

GEARING BY WHICH TABLE IS MOVED

CAMERA

MINIATURE SET

CIRCULAR REVOLVING TABLE WHICH MOVES SET IN FRONT OF LENS

© Fleischer Studio

**Stereoptical Process**

Illustrated here is the three-dimensional Stereoptical process developed by Max Fleischer in 1934. It involved positioning cel animation cartoon characters in front of three-dimensional models in order to create movement and give an illusion of greater depth and detail.

plans, due largely to corporate reorganization, Fleischer's production of the longer-format Popeye specials was used as a gradual transition to features, beginning with *Popeye the Sailor Meets Sinbad the Sailor* (1936) and *Popeye the Sailor Meets Ali Baba and His Forty Thieves* (1937). These full Technicolor specials, using the three-dimensional Stereoptical process, suggested the possibilities of what could be done by Fleischer in full-length animated features. But this was never quite realized.

## Fine Features

The phenomenal success of Disney's *Snow White* proved that animated features were big at the box office, and Paramount wanted one for a 1939 Christmas release. Several concepts such as *Peter Pan*, *The Blue Bird* and *Neptune's Daughter* (*The Little Mermaid*) were considered. Finally, *Gulliver's Travels* was pressed into production. Disney had spent over $1 million, with three years of development and 18 months of production, but Fleischer was given only 18 months and $500,000 for the entire development and final delivery. Fleischer Studios moved to Miami, Florida, but relocation expenses drove the production costs to $1 million, schedules were rushed with no time for retakes, and relations with Technicolor were strained due to missed deadlines. Miraculously *Gulliver* met its premier date and earned an impressive amount at the box office. It did not, however, make a profit. And with the war in Europe starting two months earlier, Paramount's foreign release outlets were closed off, leaving *Gulliver* $500,000 in the red. Fleischer's second, and better, feature, *Mr Bug Goes to Town* (1941) was produced on budget, but was another victim of World War Two's escalation. *Mr Bug* was released just two days before the bombing of Pearl Harbor, and the film's general theatrical release was delayed.

Two years earlier, Universal offered Walter Lantz $700,000 to produce a version of *Aladdin and His Wonderful Lamp*. Lantz had just completed the storyboards, but hearing of Fleischer's problems in Florida, he abandoned the project. Fleischer's efforts in competing with Walt Disney became the victim of unfortunate fate. Had events been different, Fleischer Studios could very well have become a serious contender for Disney in the feature arena.

# HAPPY HARMONIES

In 1934, Hugh Harman and Rudolf Ising moved their affiliation from Warner Bros. to Metro-Goldwyn-Mayer, as MGM offered them higher budgets and the chance to make films in color. Since their last names formed a pun on "harmonising", Harman and Ising called their new series *Happy Harmonies*.

## Fairy Tale Magic

The *Happy Harmonies* were similar to Disney's *Silly Symphonies* in that each cartoon usually featured new characters and had the feeling of a fairy tale. Rudy Ising's *The Calico Dragon* (1935) transformed a child's bed into a battlefield for a toy knight and dragon. Hugh Harman's *Bottles* (1936) took place in a pharmacy where bottles came to life and their personalities mirrored their functions; baby bottles acted like spoiled brats, and a bottle of poison was a villain.

Not every cartoon featured new characters. Harman continued to use the star of the *Looney Tunes* series, Bosko, in cartoons like *Bosko's Parlor Pranks* (1934) and *Hey, Hey Fever* (1935). For later Bosko cartoons such as *Circus Daze* (1937) and *Bosko in Baghdad* (1938), Harman made the character into a more realistic-looking black boy. Ising made several cartoons starring a mouse that first appeared in *Little Cheezer* (1936). He also created a pair of puppies for *Two Little Pups* (1936), *The Pups' Christmas* (1936) and *Wayward Pups* (1937).

## A Second Wind

The *Happy Harmonies* were lavish-looking cartoons. In addition to color, they were filled with animated shadows, reflections, special effects and animated backgrounds. However, when Harman and Ising's contract expired in 1937, MGM decided not to renew it. Instead, in an attempt to save money, MGM created its own cartoon studio and hired many of Harman and Ising's artists. They also lured director Friz Freleng away from Warner Bros. and brought in newspaper cartoonist Milt Gross. Fred Quimby, a former film salesman, was chosen to run the studio.

**Peace on Earth – soldier**

The plot of *Peace on Earth* involves two squirrel children asking their grandfather about humans. He narrates the chilling story of how humanity destroyed itself through war, leaving animals to live in peace forever.

**Peace on Earth**

Nominated for an Academy Award, in 1940 *Peace on Earth* also became the only cartoon ever to be nominated for the Nobel Peace Prize.

© Metro-Goldwyn-Mayer

*Silly Symphonies* » 36   *Looney Tunes* » 42

To escape the impending Nazi rise to power, Fischinger accepted a contract offer from Paramount Pictures to go to Hollywood and work in their special effects department. He completed *Allegretto* in 1936 with diamonds and circles whirling about in color to the music. Originally conceived as a preface to their feature *The Big Broadcast of 1937*, Paramount never used this segment because color proved too costly. He moved on to MGM, creating a short, *An Optical Poem*, in 1938.

Fischinger's approach of blending music with animation inspired the artists and animators on Walt Disney's *Fantasia* (1940), and Oskar was hired by Walt to work on the "Toccata and Fugue" sequence. He only lasted there nine months before leaving the studio.

His involvement with the major Hollywood studios ended. Oskar Fischinger decided instead to concentrate on painting and personal films.

### Muratti Privat

In this 1935 commercial, Fischinger used the patterns of cigarettes to create optical effects with Mozart's Turkish Rondo as a soundtrack. The patterns ranged from checkerboard patterns of cigarette packages to a scene in which rows of cigarettes join together in pairs which wave at the audience as if they were the legs.

### Studie Nr. 6

By 1922 Fischinger had begun to produce abstract films, and in a few years was synchronizing abstract imagery to popular records with a series he called Studies. These films were shown in theaters as advertisements for the recordings. Sixty years before MTV, they were the first music videos. Each of these studies ran three minutes in length and included approximately 5,000 drawings coordinated to the music.

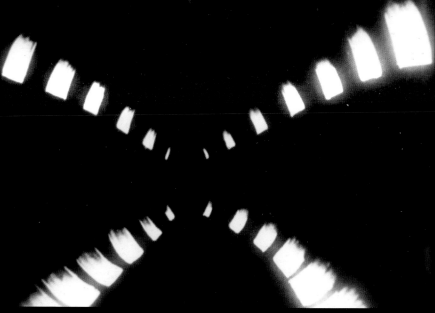

III: 1934–39: TECHNICOLOR FANTASIES   WESTERN EUROPE: GERMANY

# GEORGE PAL

Hungarian György Marczincsák (George Pal) made a unique contribution to the chronicles of fantasy films by using model animation, or Puppetoons as he christened them, in place of the traditionally drawn medium.

© Estate of George Pal/Arnold Leibovit Entertainment

### Early Life

Pal initially trained as a draftsman, subsequently working in a Budapest advertising company, where he learned his animation trade along with his young assistant, János Halász (John Halas). After a couple of years of turning out cut-out animation for commercials, in 1930 he shifted to Berlin as a set designer for Universum Film, A.G. (UFA), the major German film production company. UFA functioned by receiving a government subsidy to produce films on German themes.

Having worked there for a couple of years, Pal found out that the Gestapo was investigating him and his fellow workers for the solitary reason that he was Hungarian. Driven out of Berlin by the Gestapo, Pal would get revenge years later with one of his madcap models, *Tulips Shall Grow* (1942), which featured a peaceful Holland being disrupted by goose-stepping robots. The robots are put out of commission when the rains come and everything returns to normal.

### Animated Commercials

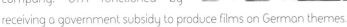

In 1933, Pal tried to set up shop in Czechoslovakia with the intention of starting up his own studio. Unable to find a cartoon camera anywhere in the country, he journeyed further afield to Paris, where he was able to form a studio. After a brief sojourn in Paris, he decided it was time to move on and, in 1934, moved to Eindhoven, Holland, where he set up a studio to make his own advertising films with partner Dave Bader. He remained there for the next five years.

He soon signed a deal with the Dutch electrical company Philips and with J. Walter Thompson, the huge advertising conglomerate representing the malted drink

**George Pal**

Born in Hungary in 1908, George Pal originally intended to train as an architect at the Budapest Academy. However, a clerical error meant that he took illustration classes and he never looked back.

**On Parade**

George Pal produced some of the most beautiful and meticulously designed films of the golden age of animation. This would serve him well in his later career as a producer of big-budget Hollywood science-fiction feature-films.

## Black and White

This early Soviet sound film by Ivanov-Vano tells the story of an old black plantation worker who questions the system in Cuba, where the black man does the hard labor while the white man takes the profits.

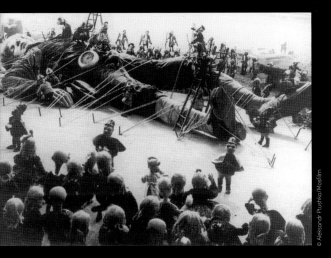

© Aleksandr Ptushko/Mosfilm

## The New Gulliver – prologue

The film begins with a live-action prologue, but the majority of the film is set in an animated Lilliput consisting of pixilated puppets and clay figures that often share the frame with the human actor playing Gulliver.

## The New Gulliver – table

The first major work by director Alexander Ptushko, *The New Gulliver* was also one of the first feature-length films to showcase puppet animation. Over 3,000 separate figures were used in this hybrid of stop-motion animation and live-action footage.

© Leonid Amalrik & Ivan Ivanov-Vano

## Ivan Ivanov-Vano and Lev Atamanov

Two other significant voices emerged during this period: Ivan Ivanov-Vano (1900–87) and Lev Atamanov (1905–81). Ivanov-Vano was one of the most popular and prolific Soviet animators. He made the satirical *Black and White* (1932), which was also among the first Soviet sound cartoons, and folkloric and children's films that included a 1938 version of *The Three Musketeers* that borrows heavily from Disney's Donald Duck character. Armenian-born Atamanov directed a series called *Ink-Spot*, along with an anti-military satire, *The Story of the Little White Bull* (1933), before moving to Armenia where he set the groundwork for Armenian animation production. By the late 1930s, Soyuzmultfilm was producing over 20 films per year and beginning to work in color.

III: 1934–39: TECHNICOLOR FANTASIES   ASIA: JAPAN & CHINA

From 1934 to 1937, Japan was officially at peace with the world. In July 1937 the Japanese Army went to war with China, and in Japan, the military openly assumed power over the government. As a result, the cinematic industry was pressured to increase sharply its production of stridently nationalistic films. Animation of the 1934–39 period continued to be monochromatic, one reel of six to 14 minutes in length. Grouped by theme, notable examples include comedies for adults, folk tales and funny animal animation, and militaristic comedies.

## Bringing Legends to Life

Usually set in the samurai era or mythical past, comedies for adults included films such as *Love in the Genroku Era: Sankichi and Osayo* by Mitsuyo Seo (1934) and *A Night at a Tavern* by Yasuji Murata (1936). Folk tales and funny animal animation were predominantly aimed at children, on the other hand, and included *The Tale of Tiny Issun Bochi's Rescue* by Mitsuyo Seo (June 1935), *Benkei versus Ushiwaka* by Kenzo Masaoka (Japan's first film animated to a prerecorded music track in July 1939) and *The Hare's Revenge on the Tanuki* (1939)by Kon Ichikawa.

**Taro Thumb – sequence 1**

Films featuring folk tales and animals aimed at children were made during the 1930s; those which took their subject matter from Japan's mythical past were primarily for adults. Pictured is Mistuyo Seo's *Taro Thumb* from 1935.

## Kon Ichikawa

The animated cartoon *The Hare's Revenge on the Tanuki* has been cited as a leading animated film of this period, but that seems due less to the film itself than to the status of Kon Ichikawa (b. 1915) as one of Japan's greatest live-action film directors of the 1950s and 1960s. Ichikawa made only one other animated film, the puppet stop-motion *The Girl at*

**Anti-Japanese War Songs**

These propaganda shorts were made during 1937 by the Wan Brothers after their studio in Shanghai was destroyed by the Japanese invasion of the city.

**Taro Thumb – sequence 2**

*Dojo's Temple* (1946), which Ichikawa has claimed as one of his greatest works. However, it was confiscated by the post-war occupation authorities and was never seen by the public.

Militaristic comedies began primarily as fantasies for children, such as *My Emergency* (ducks and frogs prepare for an air raid) by Sanae Yamamoto (1936) and *Maabo, the Boy Pilot* (1937) by Ginjiro Sato. These frequently featured themes of civil defense against foreign aggression. By 1938, the animation was aimed more toward adults and was more supportive of an "aggressive defense". *Skies over the Shanghai Battlegrounds* (1938) features two comedic Japanese pilots observing their army's successful advance around Shanghai, while in *Aerial Ace* (1938) by Noburo Ofuji, a funny animal pilot in a toy fighter plane with Japanese military markings is menaced by giant clouds in the forms of Popeye and Stalin.

## China: Temporarily Missing in Action

The Wan Brothers created numerous animated shorts for the Mingxing Film Company utilizing cartoon and cut-paper animation, sometimes mixed with live action. The most notable was *The Camel's Dance* (1935), China's first sound cartoon. Many of these, such as *Detective Dog* and *The Tortoise and the Hare*, were funny animal comedies for children, and although there was no attempt to create starring characters, some of the animals were recognizably repeating characters.

When the Mingxing studio was destroyed during the Japanese capture of Shanghai in August 1937, the Wans relocated to Wuhan province, where they made patriotic animation such as *The Anti-Japanese War Special Collection*, *Slogans of the Anti-Japanese War* and *Songs of the Anti-Japanese War* for the China Film Production Firm. These were not commercially successful. In 1939, Wan Lai-ming and Wan Gu-chan accepted an invitation from the Xinhua United Film Company in the French concession in Japanese-occupied Shanghai to set up an animation studio. They returned just in time to see Disney's *Snow White and the Seven Dwarfs* playing in Shanghai. This inspired them to begin a similar Chinese animated feature. The result was China's first full-length cartoon, *Princess with the Iron Fan* (1941).

## 1940–44:
# THE WORLD WAR TWO ERA

The world went to war — and animation went with it. The Hollywood studios were drafted and created hundreds of training films for the army — and patriotic propaganda for the home front. Daffy Duck, Mickey Mouse and Popeye fought the enemy and sold war bonds. The "wise guy" character was in vogue: Bugs Bunny, Woody Woodpecker, Screwy Squirrel. And Disney made his greatest features: *Fantasia*, *Dumbo* and *Bambi*.

Character animation hit its zenith. Animated shorts were slick and professional, but generally conformed to the Disney school of cartooning. However, a new school began to form. Creative thinkers like John Hubley, Chuck Jones and Frank Tashlin emerged and began to hint at a new direction for animation design.

But the war kept everyone, everywhere, occupied. China and Russia began creating animated films to bring ancient fables to life. Germany and Japan used cartoons for Axis wartime propaganda, as Great Britain and Canada aided the Allied troops with the same.

It was a time of shortages and sacrifice, crisis and conflict. Animators reached into their arsenal and achieved victory. Mission accomplished. Animation art was in its prime.

Between 1940 and 1944, the Disney studio's total output was great, but its nature was considerably altered because of World War Two. The rise of fascist power hindered and often curtailed European distribution of all US films, and so Disney was kept afloat largely through government projects, from propaganda and training films to Latin American health films. These projects allowed Disney to retain a greater percentage of his artists, who were therefore exempted from the draft (although animators, such as Frank Thomas, left to join the armed forces anyway). Like those of Warner Bros. and others, Disney's 1940s short subjects were thus dominated by wartime sensibilities.

**Der Fuehrer's Face**

Produced by Disney to help the American war effort and the only Donald Duck film to win an Academy Award, *Der Fuehrer's Face* (1943) featured Donald as a worker in a munitions factory dreaming of freedom in Nazi Germany.

## Patriot Donald

Mickey Mouse began to decrease in screen prominence, despite making a few notable appearances, particularly as the harried maestro in *Symphony Hour* (1942). By 1944, he appeared only in support to Pluto, apart from a cameo in *Out of the Frying Pan, Into the Firing Line* (1942) and an appearance in a parade in *All Together* (1942). He also had no role in film propaganda, despite fighting the Nazis in the newspaper strip. This more passive and suburbanized Mickey was therefore overshadowed by Donald Duck, whose easily stirred emotions and general good intentions allowed him variously to represent the American soldier, the taxpayer/citizen, or even the victim of German cruelty.

As a soldier, Donald served the US through typical army antics in several shorts with Sgt. Pete, reminiscent of Abbott and Costello's live-action comedies such as *Buck Privates* (1941). His patriotism was channeled towards promoting taxes and war bonds in a pair of shorts for the US Treasury, *The New Spirit* (1942) and *The Spirit of '43*. In the Oscar-winning *Der Fuehrer's Face* (1943), Donald endures life in a nightmarish "Nutziland", which is both satirically amusing (aided by the title song, a Spike Jones rendition, already a hit with wartime audiences) and truly horrific, as he is starved and driven insane by his German taskmasters. Waking from his dream at the end, Donald's patriotism is reaffirmed as he embraces the Statue of Liberty.

## Serving Their Country

Pluto and Goofy also served the war effort, with Pluto promoting fat conservation and serving in the army in several shorts. Goofy saved gas on the home front in *Victory Vehicles* (1943) and shattered the Rising Sun in the climax of *How to Be a Sailor* (1944). However, in 1943, Disney also produced three "psychological" propaganda shorts, representing some of the most atypical and complex films to come from the studio. *Education for Death* combines a fairly straight documentary examination of Nazi indoctrination with a brief German version of *Sleeping Beauty*, with Prince Hitler and Democracy as the witch. *Reason and Emotion* is even more complex, as the ego and the

**Der Fuehrer's Face**

After a frantic workday trying to alternate between making bombs and saluting Hitler, Donald realizes that it has all been a nightmare and that he is safely back in the good old USA.

## Gremlins – sketch

Based on Roald Dahl's 1943 book *The Gremlins*, Disney's staff started work on a wartime feature film about gremlins who foiled British pilots. Much work was done on the film, like this story sketch above – and Disney even produced some merchandizing to promote its production – before the project was abandoned.

id, represented as the title characters (the former a bespectacled prude and the latter a caveman) struggle to control man's mind, and are susceptible to enemy propaganda. *Chicken Little* uses the old fable again to denounce propaganda and rumors, and ends with the fox consuming everyone. These three shorts demonstrate the true power of animation to convey messages and stir emotion, and had more in common with the Disney features than the earlier Mickey Mouse shorts.

# DISNEY'S WARTIME FEATURES

Although Disney's short-production rates remained high due to government projects, World War Two greatly hindered Walt's feature-film plans. *Pinocchio* and especially *Fantasia* (both 1940) were less successful than expected due to high production costs and lack of foreign markets. Thus, plans for a number of film projects were considerably delayed and altered. However, between 1940 and 1944, Disney did complete production of two films, which are arguably among his greatest (*Dumbo* and *Bambi*), and three cheaper films notable for their experimentation with live footage and the way they reflect the situations at the studio and abroad (*The Reluctant Dragon*, *Saludos Amigos* and *Victory Through Air Power*).

### The Reluctant Dragon

*The Reluctant Dragon* (1941), in contrast to the ambitious *Fantasia*, was an inexpensive feature relying heavily on live-action footage of humorist Robert Benchley touring the studio. This pseudo-documentary format is entertaining, but misleading, as not only were real animators like Ward Kimball (1914–2002) juxtaposed against Alan Ladd as a storyboard artist, but the studio was undergoing a major strike at the time. Among the film's highlights is the limited-animation "Baby Weems" segment, with caricatures of Einstein and FDR, and glimpses of art and preview sequences for planned films, including *Bambi* and *Dumbo*'s Casey Jr. In one scene, a row of maquettes showcases Captain Hook, Peter Pan and Aunt Sarah and the Siamese cats from *Lady and the Tramp*, which would be sidelined for more than 10 years due to the financial setbacks of the war and the trend toward "package films" combining shorts and live action, which *Reluctant Dragon* exemplified.

### Dumbo

*Dumbo* (1941) was also inexpensive, but succeeded as more than a mere novelty film. Running a little over an hour, the tale of the baby elephant with big ears and his path from ridicule to success has a charming Horatio Alger quality, as well as a lively circus atmosphere. Disney and Fleischer veteran Grim Natwick (1890–1990), in a June 1979 *Cartoonist Profiles* article, stated: "(It is) a long short. It has the effervescent tempo of the shorts and the physical stature of a feature film."

The warmth in the animation of Dumbo and his mother by Vladimir Tytla (1904–68), along with the lively songs and surreal "Pink Elephant" march, has charmed audiences for decades. The film's closing montage includes a quick shot of Dumbo-style

© The Walt Disney Company

**Saludos Amigos**

Inspired by a trip to South America undertaken by several Disney artists, *Saludos Amigos* was one of the first in a series of "Good Neighbor" films made by Disney at the request of the Office of Inter-American Affairs. It consisted of four cartoons linked by live-action travel footage.

**Dumbo – storyboard**

Winning an Academy Award for Best Music in 1941, *Dumbo* was hugely popular on its release and it has remained a favorite ever since. Its low cost and popular appeal resulted in a much-needed financial success for Disney.

**Dumbo –sketch and cel**

Although something of a departure for Disney following the labor-intensive *Snow White*, *Pinocchio* and *Fantasia*, the gamble paid off. The film was simple and succinct and one of Disney's shortest animated features at just 64 minutes, and many believe that this set it apart from its more "arty" predecessors.

bomber planes, thereby acknowledging the war. A few months later, *Dumbo* was followed by *Mr. Bug Goes to Town* (1941), the second (and last) feature from the Fleischer brothers, and the only significant non-Disney American animated feature until the 1950s.

## Bambi

*Bambi* (1942), based on the Felix Salten book, was more ambitious, and the animation veered more toward realism than caricature. As with *Dumbo*, however, the mother-child relationship is emotionally affecting, and colorful side characters like Thumper and Friend Owl are subtly interwoven into the coming-of-age story. The lush effects animation during the "April Showers" sequence is particularly atmospheric as the various animals scuttle for shelter. Pure narrative animated films at Disney, displaced by package features, would not be seen again until *Cinderella* (1950), but *Dumbo* and *Bambi* would not be equaled.

## Wartime Experimentation

*Saludos Amigos* (1943) was one of two "Good Neighbor Policy" films, along with *Three Caballeros* (1945), that showcased Latin America. Not only did they provide another market for the films, but they also aided crucial foreign relations during wartime. *Saludos Amigos* contained travelogue footage of Disney and his crew in South America, framing four cartoon shorts, some of which involved Goofy, new character Jose Carioca, and Donald Duck, already established as a wartime icon at home.

Finally, in 1943 Disney produced the seldom-seen but fascinating *Victory Through Air Power*. This mix of documentary and military theory was not funded by the government, but was Walt's own idea, having been impressed by the theories of aviator Major Alexander de Seversky (1894–1974) and his emphasis on strategic air bombing. Live footage of de Seversky presenting his theories, surrounded by maps and a globe, is coupled with animated sequences utilizing limited character animation and moving diagrams, resembling the stylized live-action maps. The wartime symbolism was even stronger than in the shorts: de Seversky's birth date is accompanied by the Statue of Liberty, and the finale depicts the American eagle defeating the Japanese octopus. Overall, despite their financial limitations, the features of the 1940s are unique and bear Walt's personal stamp more closely than later films, when theme-park development, television and live-action films occupied more of his time and interest.

# DAFFY DUCK & BUGS BUNNY

With three simple words – "What's up, Doc?" – a new era in Warner Bros.' cartoon history had begun. Whilst Bugs Bunny had appeared in previous cartoons, it was in Tex Avery's *A Wild Hare* (1940) that the Bugs we know today made his definitive first appearance. A powerhouse team of talented directors, each possessing different yet complementary strengths was ready to make the funniest cartoons ever made. Tex Avery, Bob Clampett, Friz Freleng and Chuck Jones were on hand to kick off this golden era, with Frank Tashlin occupying Avery's chair by 1942. The confluence of a talented group of animators, working with fresh, new characters against the backdrop of a war effort that the whole studio seemed enthusiastically to embrace, made the war years an exciting time for the studio.

## Patriotic Feeling

It is worth pointing out that, while some of the other Hollywood studios were hesitant to mix politics with business before Pearl Harbor, Warner Bros. had reason early on to take a stand against Nazi Germany. The studio had closed its German distribution office in the late 1930s after a Warner representative was beaten to death by Nazi thugs. Warner's feature division declared war long before the US government did, with the 1939 release of the feature film *Confessions of a Nazi Spy*.

The Warner animation division was not the only cartoon shop to reference the war via cartoons, but few got involved as early or with the intensity of patriotic fervor found in the Warner cartoons. Who else but Daffy Duck would have the nerve to smack Hitler in the face with a mallet? Bob Clampett explained that Bugs Bunny was "a symbol of America's resistance to Hitler and the fascist powers ..." This was a remarkable time indeed for new characters to be created.

### Bugs Bunny

Wisecracking rabbit Bugs Bunny is arguably one of the most popular and recognizable cartoon characters ever created. For many years he was voiced by Mel Blanc, who gave him a distinctive Brooklyn accent.

© Halas & Batchelor

### Dustbin Parade

*Dustbin Parade*, made in 1941, about recycling materials for munitions, was one example of the 70 artful but highly engaging cartoon films made by the studio addressing domestic, government and military needs.

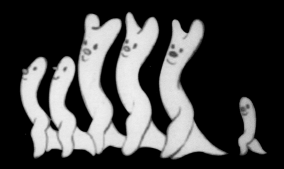

### Dustbin Parade – iron

Recognizing animated films' capacity to educate as well as entertain, the Ministry of Information invited Halas and Batchelor to create wartime public information and propaganda shorts, such as *Dustbin Parade* (pictured).

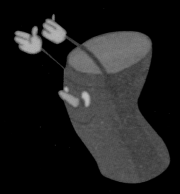

## Festival of Britain

In 1951 the studio embarked on its most ambitious project to date, bringing to the screen a faithful representation of George Orwell's cautionary tale *Animal Farm*, about animals revolting and taking over a farm. It was a project that dominated the studio for three years.

On the crest of the success of Britain's first feature cartoon, the team returned to the business of making animated cartoons and experimenting with paper sculpture in *The Figurehead* (1953), the three-dimensional in *The Owl and the Pussycat* (1953) and Cinerama in *Cinerama Holiday* (1955). The studio continued to make commercial, instructional, industrial and children's entertainment films, winning many awards and nominations along the way.

## Commercial Success

With the advent of commercial television in 1955, Halas and Batchelor jumped straight into the medium and were the first to make TV commercials, and later children's series such as *Foo-Foo* (1959), *Snip and Snap* (1960), *Do-Do the Kid from Outer Space* (1964) and *Tales of Hoffnung* (1965), which interpreted the humor of popular British cartoonist Gerard Hoffnung. Amid their colossal output, time was somehow found for another feature, *Ruddigore or the Witch's Curse* (1967), an animated representation of Gilbert and Sullivan's libretto.

Always a little ahead of the others, Halas and Batchelor moved into the computer age before others realized that computer animation was the future.

# DAVID HAND & BRITISH ANIMATION

July 1944 heralded the arrival of the noted animator and director David Dodd Hand (1900–86) to England's shores. He had been brought over to launch a British animation studio for the J. Arthur Rank Organization in the expectation of rivaling the American market in pure entertainment films. New Jersey-born Hand had been a veteran of the cartoon field since 1919, commencing his career by animating on the very basic *Andy Gump* series, filtering through the Bray Studios and finally settling at the Walt Disney Studios in 1930. His crowning glory came when Walt Disney asked him to direct the first full-length animated feature, *Snow White and the Seven Dwarfs* (1937).

## Founding an Industry

The war was still rife in Europe when Hand first sailed to England to investigate the possibilities of creating a cartoon industry over an eight-week period, and with a budget of just $8,000. It had been decided that war-torn London would be out of the question for a studio, but then he discovered Moor Hall, a sumptuous Victorian mansion in the idyllic setting of the Berkshire village Cookham-on-Thames. This was the base that trained and housed many of the staff while London was reeling with severe war damage and housing shortages. The end product had the lengthy title of Gaumont-British Animation, Ltd. (GBA).

One of the first priorities was to start a training school, and for this he brought over three highly competent ex-Disney employees on a three-year contract: story man Ralph Wright, effects animator John Reed and animator Ray Patterson. Cameraman Bill Garity (later to become Walter Lantz's right-hand man) was also brought over to help set up the camera department. Extensive advertising encouraged many young hopefuls fresh from art school and the services to train as directors, story men, animators, paint mixers, camera operators, inkers and painters, etc., culminating in nearly 200 employees involved in a four-year training schedule.

The manor's old coach house was converted into a camera department, air-raid shelters became a review theater and recording studio, and a model stage was built on to the library. Two basic units were established: one to tend to instructional demands, and the other, captained by Bert Felstead, to produce a series of entertainment cartoons for theatrical distribution. These were essentially the *Animaland* and the *Musical Paintbox* series.

## Varied Output

Throughout this duration, GBA was also responsible for many instructional cartoons on subjects as varied as blood circulation and digestion, to an account of the Magna Carta, alongside commercials ranging from Oxydol to Rowntree's Cocoa.

**David Hand (center) with Ralph Wright**

David Hand set up the animation studio at Moor Park with the aim of producing a regular series of cartoon films to entertain and, above all, to be British in character and humor. Sadly, the plan floundered and plans for feature-length cartoon versions of Lewis Carroll's poem 'The Hunting of the Snark' and H. G. Wells' *The First Men in the Moon* were shelved.

© Gaumont-British Animation Ltd (GBA)

**The Lion**

Hand's *Animaland* series included *The Lion*. Hand was supervising director on Disney's *Snow White* and *Bambi*, so it is no surprise that the characters featured in these shorts bear some resemblance, although they are perhaps zanier and more adventurous, to Snow White and Bambi's woodland friends.

**The Platypus**

Hand and his team tried to develop a new style rather than just mimic Disney, with clever plots, strange characters and surreal settings. Most of the *Animaland* shorts had minimal dialogue, but when the characters did speak, they often had British accents. Some were introduced by an off-screen British narrator, who would give "scientific" information about the lead animal, such as the platypus (pictured).

*Snow White and the Seven Dwarfs* » 58  Halas and Batchelor » 104

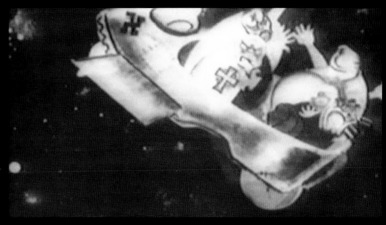

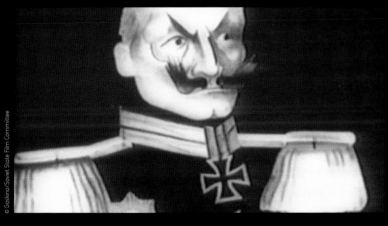

**The Interplanetary Revolution**

Another Ivan Ivanov-Vano Communist propaganda short made before the war, this was a cartoon parody of the Soviet film *Aelita* in which three Soviets fly to Mars. There a love affair develops between the Martian queen, Aelita, and one of the Soviet men while a revolution takes place on the planet.

## Soyuzmultfilm

For the most part, animation production in Eastern Europe and the USSR — what there was of it — came to a complete stop during World War Two. However, the Soviet State animation studio, Soyuzmultfilm (founded in 1936), continued to produce an assortment of fairy tales and propaganda films during this period.

Following the Nazi invasion of the USSR in 1941, Soyuzmultfilm made patriotic animated short films with titles like *Not to Stamp Fascist Boots on Our Homeland* (1941) by Ivan Ivanov-Vano and *Vultures* (1941) by Pantilemon Sazonov. The first is a black-and-white film highlighted by a rousing rendition of a popular patriotic marching song "Our Armor Is Strong and Our Tanks Are Fast", and the latter, *Vultures*, is about those German "fascist vultures".

These shorts and others like them — many of which have not survived — were shown in cinemas across the Soviet Union. Because of the urgency of the messages, the ideas for these films were born on the spot and created very fast. Many of the animators actually felt that they were being mobilized like soldiers, that they were obligated to make these films. And in fact they were. But the animators also tried to inject these films with ingenuity and enthusiasm.

Shortly after the war began, those not mobilized into the army were sent to Samarkand, a desert city in Uzbekistan. Work continued at the studio, but many major projects were put on hold and completed only after the war.

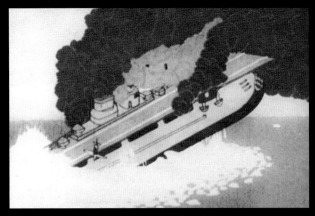
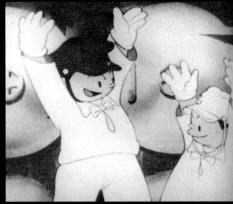

© Tadahito Mochinaga

Japanese animation from 1940 through to the end of World War Two was almost totally devoted to domestic military propaganda. The Imperial Navy fully supported this with funding and scarce production supplies, and deferral from military service for animators.

## Something for Everyone

There was plenty of live-action cinematic propaganda for adults, so the animated shorts tended to be aimed at families and children. Two cartoons that glorified the Imperial Navy with heroic little boy submarine crews and fighter pilots were *Ma-bo's Paratroop Unit* (1943) by Ginjiro Sato and *Fuku-chan and the Submarine* by Tadahito Mochinaga (1919–99), released in November 1944.

After December 1941, when Japan added America and Britain to its foes, caricatures of Anglo-enemy leaders became common. Little-boy and funny animal soldiers and sailors bravely stood up to menacing giant lampoons of Roosevelt, Churchill and Chiang Kai-shek, who cravenly ran away when stood up to.

### Fuku-chan and the Submarine

This 1944 film by Tadahito Mochinaga featured Fuku-chan, one of one of Japan's most popular newspaper comic-strip characters, and was intended to boost patriotism. There were severe food shortages at the time, the abundant food supply in the submarine kitchen was prepared into various dishes along with a merry, rhythmic song.

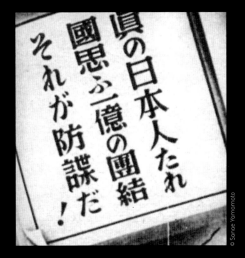

© Sanae Yamamoto

### Spies Defeated

Made in order to boost morale amongst the Japanese population, Sanae Yamamoto's 1942 film saw British and American spies caught soon after they are sent to Japan.

### The Spider and the Tulip

This film was made in 1942 using real flowers, and a cartoon spider and ladybird. It has been called anti-Western, and has been seen as political protest, with the tulip/ladybird representing the Japanese population and the spider symbolizing the American invaders, who gets its comeuppance when it is blown away by a storm.

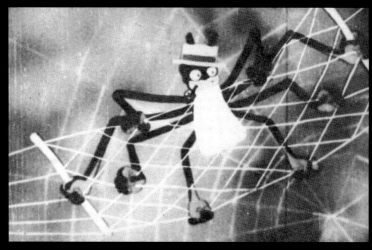

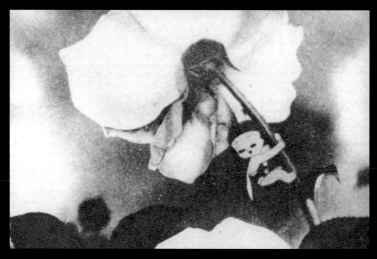

## War Leaders Vilified

In Sanae Yamamoto's *Spies Defeated* (1942), Roosevelt and Churchill send spies into Japan who are quickly captured. Ryoji Mikami's *Hooray for Japan!* (1943) combines live-action exhortations to support the war effort with animated political cartoon exaggerations of the quick defeat of the British Army and Navy in December 1941 to early 1942, and a caricature of Chiang Kai-shek as an incompetent puppet of the Americans and British. Mitsuyo Seo's 1933 monkey soldier Sankichi returned, redesigned to look less humorous and more dramatic, in two films by Kotaro Kataoka: *Sankichi the Monkey's Marine Corps Air Defense* (1941) and *Sankichi the Monkey's Fighting Submarine* (July 1943).

The little fine-art animation that there was during this period was dominated by two animators, Kazugoro Arai (b. 1907) and Kenzo Masaoka (1898–1988). Kazugoro Arai was a dentist whose hobby was animation of delicate, stately silhouette cut-outs in the style of Japanese shadow puppetry. He produced two romances set in ancient Japan, *Fantasy of the Butterfly Wife* (1940) and *Princess Kaguya* (1942), and also *Jack and the Beanstalk* (1941). He was then swept up into the propaganda animation production, contributing to *Hooray for Japan!* and *Momotaro's Sea Eagles*.

## The Spider and the Tulip

In 1940 Kenzo Masaoka set up a small, independent animation study programme. In 1941 he was hired by Shochiku Films to add it to its animation department. With Shochiku's resources, Masaoka produced the lovely art film *The Spider and the Tulip* during late 1942, released April 1943. A little girl ladybird playing happily in a flowery forest is menaced by a spider with a black face, wearing a Western-style straw hat. This film was not anti-Western per se, however, since such straw hats were a standard Japanese stage and movie prop for low-class buffoons and hoodlums. The spider tries to lure the ladybird, which is hidden from him by a friendly tulip. But the spider is not fooled, and is prying her out of the tulip when a violent storm breaks out. The spider's desperate attempts to keep from being swept away are so courageous that he wins the audience's sympathy, but he ultimately fails, leaving the ladybird to emerge safely when the storm ends. *The Spider and the Tulip* has a lush prerecorded score by an 80-piece orchestra. It was both a popular and a critical sensation, and is still cited by some critics as Japan's finest animated film.

# THE FIRST ANIMATED FEATURES

In 1939, Mitsuyo Seo joined the Geijutsu Eigaha (Art Film Company) that produced short animated films for the Ministry of Education, with Tadahito Mochinaga as his assistant. For their *Ant Boy* (1941), Mochinaga devised Japan's first multiplane camera. In late 1942 the Imperial Navy assumed patronage of the studio and commissioned Seo to create longer and more impressive propaganda films. Seo produced the 37-minute *Momotaro's Sea Eagles* (1943) in three months. This restaged the attack on Pearl Harbor with Momotaro as a little boy commander of a monkey and rabbit naval force dive-bombing "Devil Island", despite the comically ineffectual defense of Popeye's Olive Oyl and Bluto.

## Impressive Results

This was so popular that the navy ordered a sequel twice as long. Seo's 74-minute *Momotaro's Divinely-Blessed Sea Warriors*, still with Mochinaga's assistance, begins with four young animal naval cadets (bear cub, puppy, monkey and pheasant) returning to their forest home to say farewell to their families and to encourage their younger siblings to support the war effort. The action cuts to the Imperial Navy as bunny sailors build an airstrip on a hot island, with elephants and proboscis monkeys dressed as Indonesian natives looking on in awe. Admiral Momotaro and the four animal buddies as his aides-de-camp arrive with a squadron of fighter planes. After several scenes of happy naval-base life (plus a brief "why we fight" sequence in silhouette animation), the squadron flies off to attack a base of slovenly British troops shown as humans with a foreign devil's horn. The British surrender is a parody of Japanese newsreel footage of the surrender of Singapore. Released in April 1945, this would be Japan's first and only animated theatrical feature until 1958. It is still considered an impressive animation production for its time and the conditions under which it was made.

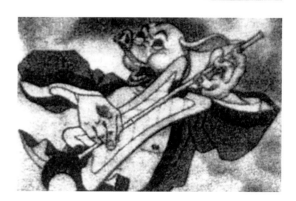

## The Wan Brothers

Greatly impressed by Disney's *Snow White and the Seven Dwarfs* (1937), the Wan Brothers threw their new Xinhua United Film animation department into the production of a feature-length adaptation of an incident from the long *Monkey King* (a.k.a. *Journey to the West*) folk tale, first written in the sixteenth century by Wu Cheng-en. On their journey to India, the Buddhist priest Tripitaka and his three supernatural bodyguards – Monkey, Pigsy and Sandy – enter a region being terrorized by demons led by a cruel buffalo-headed king who controls fire, and his wife, a princess with a magic iron fan that creates freezing cold. Monkey must defeat her and steal her fan to put out the fires and liberate the villagers.

© Ryoji Mikami

## The Chinese Snow White

The 76-minute *Princess Iron Fan* (or *Princess with the Iron Fan*) was produced in 16 months by a team of 237 artists. The cartoon animation was heavily Rotoscoped to speed production and increase the quality. Advantage was taken of the protection of the French concession from the Japanese occupation of the rest of Shanghai to draw parallels between the sadistic demons and the Japanese oppression of the Chinese people. It was released in mid- or late 1941 in unoccupied China and in Chinese communities throughout Southeast Asia to great acclaim.

After the Japanese declaration of war against the Western powers in December 1941, the French concession of Shanghai was abolished. The Wan Brothers left for Hong Kong to work on artistic projects outside of animation for the rest of the war.

**Hooray for Japan!**

Another propaganda film made in 1943, Ryoji Mikami caricatures Chiang Kai-shek as a puppet of the British and Americans.

**Princess with the Iron Fan**

Working under adverse financial and technical conditions, the Wan brothers developed an original style based on the use of clay and human models to trace movements and action. *Princess with the Iron Fan*'s plot is adapted freely from part of *Journey to the West*, an epic sixteenth-century romance that recounts the hardships and adventures of the Tang Dynasty monk Tripitaka and his disciples on their travels in search of Buddhist scriptures.

The Japanese authorities released *Princess with the Iron Fan* in Japan (minus the obviously anti-Japanese scenes) in early 1942, where it was equally popular. It was an acknowledged influence on the Imperial Navy's decision to authorize Seo's production of the 1943 and 1945 Momotaro films. Osamu Tezuka later credited seeing *Princess with the Iron Fan* when he was 13, and the Momotaro feature when he was 16, as inspiring him to become a cartoonist and animator. Tezuka's 1950s comic-book adaptation of the Monkey King legend, produced by Toei Animation in 1960 as its third animated feature, is a remake of this same story.

## Creativity Cut Off

Other Chinese animators had just begun production in 1941 before they were brutally cut short by the war. Qian Jia-jun (b. 1916), who would become prominent in the 1960s, finished his first cartoon animation that year, *The Happiness of Peasants*. In August the Chinese Cartoon Association was created in the British colony of Hong Kong. It only produced one cartoon, *The Hunger of the Old Stupid Dog*, before the Japanese occupation of Hong Kong. There was no other Chinese animation until 1947.

## 1945–49:
# THE POST-WAR ERA

A return to normality, that is if you can call a Tex Avery cartoon normal. Tex, Hanna-Barbera, Shamus Culhane, Chuck Jones and Friz Freleng all strengthened their considerable skills, and Hollywood cartoons got sharper and funnier as a baby boom began. Heckle and Jeckle, Casper the Friendly Ghost, Foghorn Leghorn and the Road Runner were the new kids on the block. And a young upstart studio, United Productions of America, began to get noticed.

Disney started to make combination live-action/animation films and expanded his artistic reach with a series of animated package films – 10-part compilation movies experimenting with different animation techniques – from surreal abstractions to literal narratives all set to current popular music.

With world markets reopened, new countries joined the animation community with ambitious feature films: France's *Mr Wonderbird*, Russia's *Magic Pony* and Italy's *Rose of Baghdad*. State-sponsored animation studios were established in Iron Curtain countries. The greatest of these was the Zagreb studio, where new ideas and personal visions were realized with freedoms otherwise impossible in the land of their creation.

A new world had begun.

# NEW DIRECTIONS FOR DISNEY

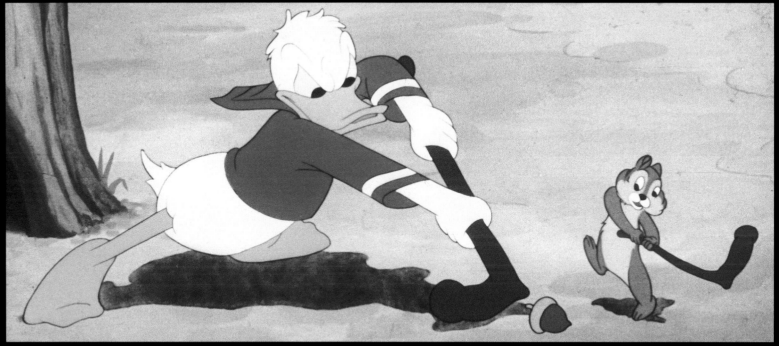

After the war, the Disney studio regrouped. Full-length narrative features, in particular, *Peter Pan*, *Alice In Wonderland* and *Lady and the Tramp*, had been on hold and time was needed to gear up to produce them. Government contracts ended, and money was tight. Disney's studio decided to play to its strength – the animated shorts.

## Starring Donald Duck

Donald Duck was Disney's biggest star. Eight Duck cartoons joined Pluto and Goofy, and an occasional Mickey or Figaro, on the RKO release schedules every year. None of them won Oscars – but many of them were quite good.

Jack King directed a trio of classics during this period: *Cured Duck* (1945), in which Daisy uses a machine to cure Donald's bad temper; *Donald's Dilemma* (1947), where a flowerpot smashed on the head provides Donald with a superior singing voice; and *Donald's Dream Voice* (1948), in which a box of pills gives Donald a distinctive, Ronald Coleman-esque enunciation.

Jack Hannah took over the series and emerged as the leading Duck auteur during this period. He moved Donald into the suburbs and built the series around his frustrations with intruding garden pests, including twin chipmunks in *Chip and Dale* (1947) and a variety of insects, including ants in *Tea for Two Hundred* (1948), bees in *Inferior Decorator* (1948) and beetles in *Bootle Beetle* (1947).

Jack Kinney made his mark as the director of a comedic series of Goofy "how-to" shorts. This led to a post-war series of hilarious sports shorts with the Goof

### Winter Storage

One of a series of Donald Duck cartoons featuring chipmunks Chip and Dale, *Winter Storage* was made in 1949. The two chipmunks are trying to find acorns for winter and take advantage of Donald's tree-planting scheme.

### Donald Duck

Donald Duck made his first appearance in 1934, supporting Mickey Mouse in *The Wise Little Hen*. He finally became the star of the show in 1937 in *Donald's Ostrich*, with his distinctive squeaky voice provided for many years by Clarence "Ducky" Nash.

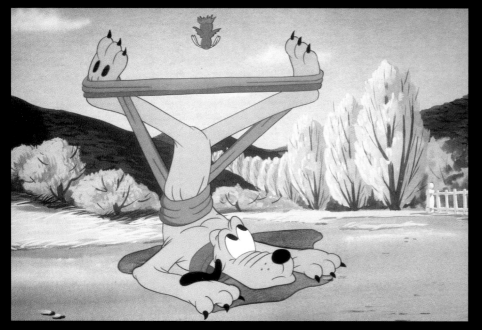

**Pluto's Fledgling**

Pluto is the star in this Disney animated short, made in 1948, in which he teaches a young bird to fly. He is more commonly featured as Mickey Mouse's sidekick, a clumsy pet dog. In his first appearance in *The Chain Gang* in 1930 he was actually one of the dogs tracking down an escaped Mickey, only becoming his faithful pet in his third animated outing, *The Moose Hunt* in 1931.

fumbling all challenges in *Hockey Homicide* (1945), *Tennis Racquet* (1949) and *Goofy Gymnastics* (1949).

## Focus on Features

Walt decided to stick with entertainment films – and canceled his contracts for industrial, commercial and educational films during this period. This was a bold move, because the studio needed income from these films. *The Dawn of Better Living* (1945), commissioned by Westinghouse Electric, and *The ABC of Hand Tools* (1946) for General Motors were typical of Disney's post-war commercial films, featuring strong visual storytelling that quickly and easily explained complicated messages – a studio speciality, learned by years of producing military training films.

Disney's *The Story of Menstruation* (1946), for Kotex, was the last commercial film the studio made for some time. This short, shown in girls' high-school hygiene classes for decades, like all Disney educational and industrial films, contains the highest standards of the studio's production values in art, animation and good taste. Though it was his strong suit, Disney knew that animated shorts were on their way out. The money was in feature production, and he had to find new ideas, and new formats, for his storytelling talents.

## Going Live

In an effort to push himself forward, Disney took a risk by releasing his first live-action short – a documentary, no less – and announced it as the first in a new series: *A Walt Disney True-Life Adventure*.

In *Seal Island* (1949), director James Algar cleverly assembled hours of live-action footage, detailing a family of Alaskan sea lions and their living habits into 27 entertaining minutes. It paid off, winning an Oscar and signaling a new direction for Disney's movie-making ambitions.

Disney had great plans for his studio, and this post-war period was a transitional time that allowed him to consider his past mistakes – and reinforce his skills.

# DISNEY MOVES ON

Between 1945 and 1949, Disney released seven feature-length films — yet none of them was a traditional animated feature-length story. Most were "package films" — feature-length collections of short segments not unlike *Fantasia* (1940), only this time the music was contemporary and popular, and the narratives were somewhat traditional.

## Spanish Style

*The Three Caballeros*, released in 1945, delayed due to restrictions on Technicolor printing, was a holdover from the South American "Good Neighbor" films Disney began during the war. This film, on the whole, is a surreal experience, with Donald Duck entering a Latin American picture book and interacting with (i.e., lusting after) a group of sexy live-action samba singers.

Surreal and Spanish also sum up Walt Disney's aborted collaboration with Salvador Dalí toward the end of 1945 and into the early part of 1946. The musical short *Destino* (abandoned, then completed in 2003) was surely an attempt to redefine what an animated film can be. But by 1946, the realities of operating a commercial studio clashed with his artistic ambitions.

## The Feature Collections

Disney knew he needed to fill his feature-film pipeline quickly — at least one film per year — so various package films were developed and live-action movies were pursued. Disney had his staff work up multiple musical scenarios for a variety of short films. These would take the place *Silly Symphonies* had held a decade earlier, and prepared his crew for more ambitious feature-length cartoons to come.

*Make Mine Music* was the first such collection, released in 1946. A collection of 10 segments, loosely bridged together, it contains a variety of visual styles and music. Popular singers and musicians including Dinah Shore, the Andrews Sisters, Nelson Eddy and Benny Goodman tell the stories of "Willie the Operatic Whale", "The Martins and the Coys", and "Casey at the Bat", among others.

© The Walt Disney Company

**Fun and Fancy Free**

This feature-length package cartoon from Disney consists of two sections: "Bongo" and "Mickey and the Beanstalk", joined together by various live-action scenes narrated by the character Jiminy Cricket.

## Output Increases

The same year, Disney released his first live-action narrative film *Song of the South* (1946). Bringing to life the American folk tales of Uncle Remus, this film incorporated three lengthy animated segments with B'rer Rabbit, B'rer Bear and B'rer Fox. The post-Civil War setting of this melodrama was controversial in its day for its portrayal of black plantation stereotypes, but regardless, it is one of Disney's finest films. Its success gave Disney the courage to pursue further live-action movies and grow his film output.

Next came *Fun and Fancy Free* (1947), which essentially tied together two tales of fantasy. "Bongo" is about a circus bear who finds love and danger in the forest, and "Mickey and the Beanstalk" is an epic Mickey Mouse, Donald Duck and Goofy adventure.

*Melody Time* (1948) was the best of the package films. Each segment is a winner: the surreal South American holdover "Blame It on the Samba" with Donald Duck; "Bumble Boogie", featuring a bee trapped in a bizarre musical landscape and set to the tune of "Flight of the Bumble Bee"; the more traditional tales of Johnny Appleseed, sung by Dennis Day; and "Pecos Bill", told by Roy Rogers.

Disney released his next live-action film *So Dear to My Heart*, in 1949 – a nostalgic tale of a boy and his pet lamb, this time with minimal (but excellent) animation segments. He ended the decade with *The Adventures of Ichabod and Mr Toad*, his last package film.

© The Walt Disney Company

## B'rer Fox

*Song of the South* featured James Baskett, who initially auditioned for a small voice part in the film. He not only got the part of Br'er Fox, but also Uncle Remus, making him the first live-action actor to be hired by Disney. Baskett also won an honorary Oscar for his efforts.

## Ichabod Crane

*The Adventures of Ichabod and Mr Toad* was the last of the package pictures of the 1940s. Money was saved during the production of packaged films by reusing animated sequences and basing characters on others that had already been drawn. As a result of this belt-tightening exercise, the Disney studio was able to finance animated features once again.

## Ichabod Crane and Mr Toad

The characters of the timid Ichabod Crane and the wild Mr Toad were two personalities the Disney crew could draw to perfection. In the feature, Kenneth Grahame's *The Wind in the Willows* is narrated by Basil Rathbone and features some of the funniest character animation the studio ever achieved. Washington Irving's *The Legend of Sleepy Hollow*,

© The Walt Disney Company

on the other hand, has one of the strongest, most unforgettable dramatic sequences in the studio's history – the spooky encounter between Ichabod and the Headless Horseman.

All of these package films experimented with animation design, and allowed Disney's character animators to explore every possible range of human emotion. Disney's team was now ready to return to full-length features.

# UPA IS FORMED

The 1941 Disney strike by the Screen Cartoonist Guild was a defining moment for American animation in more ways than one. It not only ended Disney's artistic and commercial hegemony, but also indirectly led to the birth of United Productions of America (UPA), the most innovative studio of the post-war era – in fact, it was often said to have been formed on the Disney picket lines. What's more, the political activism behind the strike carried over into an aesthetic activism that proved heavily influential for years to come.

### Developing Style

The company was formally established in 1944 as Industrial Films and Poster Service by Dave Hilberman, Zachary A. "Zach" Schwartz and Stephen Bosustow to produce *Hell Bent for Election* for the United Auto Workers (UAW) on behalf of Roosevelt's re-election campaign. Its production had been brokered by the union's business agent and largely utilized talent from other studios, especially from Warner Bros., which donated time to the effort and also director Chuck Jones. However, it was storyboarded by John Hubley, Phil Eastman and Bill Hurtz. In terms of design, it owed much to earlier Jones cartoons such as *The Dover Boys* (1942), which was among several films of the period that had decisively broken away from Disney and exhibited a more modern look. It was this type of stylization that was to develop way beyond what Jones had done and became the hallmark of UPA. Their films tended to use limited animation and put more emphasis on graphic elements such as design and color.

**Hell Bent for Election**

Many animators were keen Franklin Roosevelt be re-elected and so a number, including Chuck Jones, gave their services for free in order that the film be made on time. Roosevelt and opponent Thomas Dewey where depicted as train: the "Win the War Special" and the "Defeatist Limited" respectively. Although the result was not as technically advanced as UPA's later work would be, it was vibrant, stylish and persuasive – and very successful.

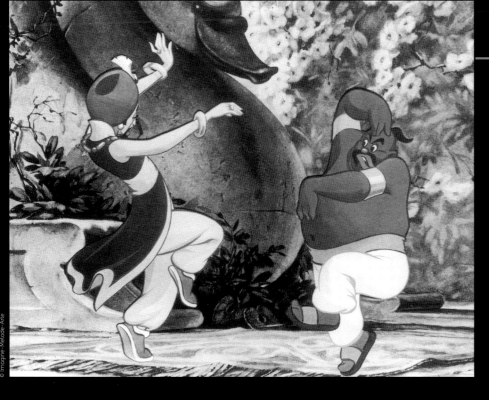

© Imagine-Melode-Arte

### La Rosa di Baghdad

Producer and director Antonio Gino Domeneghini had to move his animation team from Milan to Bornato, in the countryside of Brescia, to escape the bombing during World War Two.

### La Rosa di Baghdad

Despite an awkward narrative progression *La Rosa di Baghdad* has some beautiful scenes, such as Princess Zeila singing as the sun sets and the final firework celebration. The film did well at the box office but Domeneghini returned to advertising after its completion.

© Imagine-Melode-Arte

## Surviving the War

With the market for advertising dying on its feet, the only way Domeneghini could manage to keep his team of skilled craftsmen above water through the Blitz was by creating this film for them to work on. They stayed engaged on this production for a stressful seven-year period, spanning much of the war. Milan being one of the chief targets for Nazi bombing, Domeneghini and his crew were forced to relocate the studio away from the city in the countryside at Bornato.

A key member of Domeneghini's team, illustrator and comic artist Angelo Bioletto (1906–87), was responsible for the character design, owing more than a passing debt to Disney's *Snow White and the Seven Dwarfs*. The atmospheric backgrounds were rendered by Libico Maraja and the music was provided by Riccardo Pick Mangiagalli.

## Arabian Nights

The story is taken from an Arabian Nights fable featuring a young flautist named Amin, whose love for the fair Princess Zeila is put to the test. The villain of the piece, the evil chamberlain Burk, plans to do away with Amin, but the flute player finally wins the day, and the heart of the princess. Other characters involved are Oman the Caliph; the Princess's uncle, Sheikh Jafar; the three wise men, Tonko, Zirco and Zizibè; and Kalinà the magpie.

Filming in Technicolor proved to be an expensive luxury. The process used was the successive exposure system. Filmed on a single black-and-white negative, the method involves three identical frames shot through blue, red and green filters. This lengthy and expensive procedure was eventually abandoned in favor of the quicker Eastman Kodak system.

*La Rosa di Baghdad* did well at the box office and won first prize at the Festival dei Ragazzi in 1949 as part of the 10th Venice Film Festival. Despite this, however, Domeneghini never returned to the world of animated feature films and re-established himself with what he knew best – making commercials.

## The Singing Princess

In 1952, an English speaking version was dubbed, featuring the teenage Julie Andrews who was fast making a name for herself as a radio singer. This version was later re-discovered in the USA when Julie was at her most popular, and got a new lease of life when reissued under the title of *The Singing Princess* (1967).

# PAUL GRIMAULT & JEAN IMAGE

The premier agent for the post-war French animation scene was Paul Grimault (1905–94). Born in a suburb of Paris, he studied art at Ecole des Arts Appliquésthe, then worked as a scene painter in a theater. After military service in 1930 he became acquainted with Jean Aurenche and Jacques Prévert, collaborating with them on a collection of various projects such as theater-set design, acting (for Groupe Octobre) and constructing advertising films.

## Introducing Gô

It was here that Grimault met producer André Sarrut. They hit it off straight away and soon united to form their own studio, Les Gémeaux, in 1936, where they successfully produced uncomplicated, hand-drawn animated commercials until the war intervened. Their first attempt at theatrical entertainment was a cartoon featuring a character named Gô and was titled *Gô Chez les Oiseaux* ('Gô Among the Birds', 1939), which enjoyed moderate success.

World War Two interrupted most people's lives, and Grimault's was no exception. The 35-year-old was drafted into the army and, having served his time, he was back at the drawing board at Les Gémeaux in 1941, where his first directorial job was to rewrite and extend his 1939 hit, *Gô Chez les Oiseaux*, which became *Les Passagers de la Grande Ourse* ('The Passengers of the Big Dipper', 1941). Also well received was 1943's enchanting *L'Epouvantail* ('The Scarecrow'), the tale of a scarecrow who befriends two birds who are being pestered by a cat.

## The Little Soldier

His turning point was when he combined forces with Jacques Prévert to bring to the screen Hans Christian Andersen's charming fable of *Le Petit Soldat* ('The Little Soldier', 1947) about the love between a toy soldier and a doll. In 1946, after a succession of popular shorts, the opportunity arose for an animated feature to be made adapting another Hans Christian Andersen tale, *The Shepherdess and the Chimney Sweep*.

## Mr Wonderbird

This new venture set sail on its unsteady course under the title of *Le Bergere et la Ramoneur* ('Mr Wonderbird', 1953) and was not without its problems. After three years work on the project and many differences with Sarrut, a court case evicted Grimault from the helm of *Le Bergere et la Ramoneur* in mid-production.

Following this upset, Grimault initiated his own studio in 1951, Les Films Paul Grimault. Here he produced animated commercials, shorts and even a live-action documentary called *La Biopsie de la Molle Osseuse* (1958), although he often left the direction side to others. In 1967 he managed to obtain the rights to *Le Bergere et la*

### Jeannot L'Intrepide

Reduced to the size of a bee, Jeannot is welcomed into Bee Land and heroically defends his bee friends from a wasp attack. The bees then help Jeannot to defeat the giant who shrank him and he regains his normal size.

### L'Epouvantail

The originality and quality of Grimault's work is evident in early films such as *L'Epouvantail* (1943), a whimsical short cartoon in which a devious cat lures a bird-loving scarecrow to his doom.

### Le Petit Soldat

Grimault's version of Hans Christian Andersen's *The Tin Soldier* was released in 1947. His graphic style tended towards curved lines, full animation and realistic settings.

© Jean Image

**Jeannot L'Intrépide**

Although a French production, *Jeannot L'Intrépide* was also released commercially in America under the name *Johnny the Giant Killer*.

© Jean Image

*Ramoneur* and proceeded to remodel it into something he could be proud of. The finished product was finally completed in 1980 and released under the title of *Le Roi et l'Oiseau* ('The King and Mr Bird').

## Jean Image

The renowned cartoon director and producer known as Jean Image began life in Budapest, christened Imre Hajdu (1911–89). He studied in Budapest's School of Decorative Art, moving further afield to Berlin. By 1932, after a brief sojourn with an advertising agency, the Hungarian native had migrated to Paris and set up shop as a commercial artist. In 1936 he journeyed across the channel to England, where he served a year-long apprenticeship at British Animated Films, rubbing shoulders with his contemporary John Halas.

Back in Paris and still working under his given name, he began working on sponsored films, branching out by making several of his own animated films in his spare time, such as *Sur Deux Notes* ('On Two Notes', 1939). Adopting the nom de plume of Jean Image in 1944, he went on to produce *Les Noirs Jouent et Gagnent* ('Black Plays and Wins', 1944), his first film under this new pen name. He continued turning out commercials at his own studios and then released his second entertainment film two years later, *Rhapsodie de Saturne* ('Saturn Rhapsody') (1946).

Image then instigated the feature cartoon *Jeannot l'Intrépide* ('Fearless Jeannot', 1950, a.k.a 'Johnny The Giant Killer') which won the Grand Prix for children's films at the 1951 Venice Film Festival. The story concerns a waif-like child who, in an attempt to save further children from a giant, calls upon help from the insect world, conquering the ogre with the assistance of bees. This fairy story is entertaining and well-executed with plenty of action and memorable scenes, particularly the bee battles and aftermath.

Yugoslavia was always an anomaly in the Cold War battle. President Josip Broz Tito, who ruled the country from 1946 until his death in 1980, managed to maintain a unique neutrality. While his government was staunchly Communist, he rejected Stalin's policy of dictating to every Communist nation. He also accepted military and economic aid from the West while refusing to be subservient to the United States. Tito's strong personality and adept political instincts also managed to keep together the disparate elements of the Yugoslavian nation, despite the national aspirations of six nominally equal republics. The country's eventual breakup after his death into the independent nations of Croatia, Montenegro, Serbia, Slovenia, Bosnia-Herzegovina, and Macedonia is testament to Tito's political skills.

## Inspirational Animation

The country's primary animation studio holds an equally rare place in animation history. Its origins can be found in the advertising industry prior to World War Two, with men like Serij Tagatz, who trained in Moscow, and the Maar brothers, who had fled Germany to escape anti-Semitism. After the war, the popular magazine editor Fadil Hadzic, who has been called the "Cocteau of Yugoslavia", almost single-handedly jump-started animation production in Zagreb, the capital of Yugoslavia's Croatian republic. He organized a group of young animators and decided that their first film would celebrate the country's unique straddling of the east-west divide. The 17-minute satirical short, *The Big Meeting*, a metaphor for Yugoslavia's split with Stalinism, inspired a generation of animators.

© Fadil Hadzic, The Big Meeting, Zagreb Film

© Nihon Doga

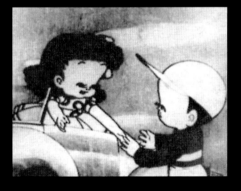

© Shin Nihon Doga Sha

animation that was pouring into Japan, along with the latest American movies that the occupation authorities brought in. The entire Japanese cinematic industry was aware that it had to modernize – and fast. This they would do in the next decade.

## China

China's wartime devastation, followed immediately by the Nationalist–Communist civil war, hampered the renaissance of Chinese animation. The first encouragement came in 1947 from Communist-controlled Northern China/Manchuria, where the Party-subsidized Tong Pei Film Studio was instructed to make animated films satirising Chiang Kai-shek's nationalist government. The puppet-animated *The Emperor's Dream* was directed by Chen Bo-er (b. 1907) and animated by Fang Ming that year, and the cartoon-animated *The Turtle Caught in the Jar* was directed and animated by Fang Ming the next year.

## Tadahito Mochinaga

Fang Ming was actually the Chinese name of Tadahito Mochinaga, Mitsuyo Seo's former assistant. He was born in Tokyo but had spent his youth in Manchuria where his father worked. Due to the increasing bombing of Japan in 1945, Mochinaga returned in June to Changchun in the puppet-nation of Manchuko to join the art department of the Manchuria Film Studio. The studio's Manchurian employees were treated as peons by the Japanese staff, and Mochinaga started a movement to demand that they all be treated equally. This won him the friendship of the Chinese, and when most of the Japanese were pressured to return to Japan after the war's end, Mochinaga was asked to remain at the renamed Tong Pei (Northeast) studio. As Fang Ming, Mochinaga became an enthusiast of Chinese-style puppet animation. After the Communist government won control over all mainland China in 1949, the cultural division assigned Te Wei (b. 1915), a print cartoonist from Shanghai, and Fang Ming to produce educational and morally uplifting animation for China's youth.

Animation also began a shaky rebirth in Hong Kong with Tan Xin Feng's 1948 puppet-animation *Prince of the Big Tree*, now lost.

# VI

## 1950–55:
# CARTOONS MATURE

United Productions of America (UPA) challenged Disney's long-held animation philosophies. With imaginative use of limited animation, modern graphics and new ideas, this small studio gained worldwide influence over the way people perceived and produced animated films.

UPA made popular modern fables, with contemporary characters, pushing the envelope artistically and creatively. And they won three Academy Awards. But Hollywood itself was undergoing a change. Widescreen CinemaScope and 3D movies were in vogue – and animation had to stretch to stay apace. At the same time, traditional animation found its greatest success. Chuck Jones made his Daffy Duck masterpieces – *Duck Dodgers, Duck Amuck* and *The Scarlet Pumpernickle* – and Disney returned to making feature-length fairy tales, including *Cinderella* and *Peter Pan*.

Disney may have had the feature-film arena to himself in the US, but in Europe new film-makers decided to compete vigorously, with ambitious productions of *Animal Farm* (Great Britain), *Mr Wonderbird* (France), and *The Snow Queen* (Russia).

Animation had found its place, and was now evolving in new directions.

It is often implied that United Productions of America (UPA) was born out of the Disney Studio strike of 1941. That event probably had something to do with bonding the original members of UPA together in some sort of alliance, but the studio would not actually come into its own until after World War Two, and the driving force would not be a strike, but a vision of animation as a modern-art form.

## First Successes

Initially, Steve Bosustow, Zack Schwartz, Dave Hilberman, John McLeish, Ted Parmelee, Phil Eastman, and especially John Hubley, formed a company called United Film Productions and found work in the burgeoning wartime animation industry. After making several films for the government, they teamed up with Warner Bros. director Chuck Jones and produced a film for Franklin Delano Roosevelt's 1944 re-election campaign, *Hell Bent for Election*. It was an immediate hit and brought a lot of attention to the small studio, now re-named United Productions of America. UPA continued to do government work, and also produced the first film that would feature the flat, graphic style that would become the studio's hallmark. *The Brotherhood of Man* (1945) was produced for the United Auto Workers to help prepare the southern states for union organization that would include racial integration. It was another success and was widely distributed beyond union meetings and community halls because of its message of tolerance and equality.

## Hollywood Under Scrutiny

World War Two ended, and the Cold War began. The FBI turned their suspicious attention to Hollywood. The UPA crew was ripe for this kind of scrutiny. Many had, after all, been instrumental in union activities and were not at all shy about their left-of-center politics. No one at UPA was charged with anything, but as the Red Scare escalated, UPA's government projects dried up.

## Mr Magoo Arrives on the Scene

The studio began to look for theatrical work to keep busy. It was at precisely this time that Columbia was searching for a new group to replace its moribund Screen Gems animation division. Bosustow, who had become UPA's executive producer, worked out a contract and the studio completed a couple of films featuring Columbia's Fox and Crow characters. They also had in mind a new character and produced a short, *Ragtime Bear* (1949), to introduce him to the public. His name was Mr Magoo, and he and his first cartoon were an immediate hit.

*Ragtime Bear* was an eye-opener for the animation industry. Daring to use bold graphics and limited animation techniques, not to save money but rather to

**Christopher Crumpet's Playmate**

This 1953 short demonstrates other aspects of limited animation: distorted perspectives; only the essential elements of the scene being present; and outlined, transparent characters. This simplified, stylized style of animation influenced the advertising industry and also the newborn medium of television.

**Mr Magoo – sketches and cel**

The creation of Quincy Magoo was inspired by a number of real-life people: the director, John Hubley's bullheaded uncle; screen comedian W. C. Fields; and Jim Backus used observations of his father when devising the voice.

## Mr Magoo – Hotsy Footsy

UPA's limited animation style was characterized by flattened perspective, abstract backgrounds and strong primary colors. Instead of filling in backgrounds with lifelike detail, broad fields of color were used, with small squiggles to suggest clouds and trees. Rather than vary the shades and hues of colors as in the natural world, UPA's cartoons used bold, bright, saturated colors.

make an artistic statement, this initial Magoo short and other UPA productions of the era stood in sharp contrast to the efforts of other animation studios, particularly Disney, for increasingly heavily articulated realism.

## Limited Animation Style

UPA's approach to limited animation relied on graphic technique, color and stylized motion to caricature the world rather than imitate it. Animation was structured into recognizable, often repeated action, with heavy emphasis placed on clear, diagrammatic design and voice performance – Magoo's success was in no small part also due to the brilliant, ad-libbed vocals of Jim Backus. To this day, no one else seems to be able to capture the befuddled, ornery confidence of his performances. The designers at UPA used this bold graphic style to its best advantage, furthering the vision best expressed by John Hubley of animation as an art form. In many ways, the artists at UPA proved architect Ludwig Mies van der Rohe's famous adage that "less is more".

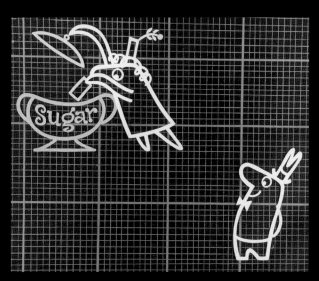

## Unicorn and Fudget's Budget

UPA's highly stylized look is exemplified in these two shorts, *Unicorn in the Garden* (1953) and *Fudget's Budget* (1954) short.

In the early 1950s, UPA's style, a departure from the traditional realistic design approach, was so influential that nearly all of the other studios began to move in this direction. Warner Bros. began to stylize their backgrounds, which was problematic in the early stages because their established characters did not particularly match. Nevertheless, films like Freleng's *Pizzicato Pussycat* (1955) and *Three Little Bops* (1957), and Chuck Jones's two Ralph Philips shorts, *From A to Z-Z-Z-Z* (1954) and *Boyhood Daze* (1957), began to reflect the new look. This continued until the studio closed.

### New Faces

*Terrytoons'* lackluster product went completely UPA with their designs for new characters like Flebus, designed by Ernest Pintof,f fresh from a stint at UPA, and Clint Clobber and Sidney the Elephant, created by Gene Deitch (b. 1924), also from UPA. Deitch's most important contribution was the wonderfully inspired television series *Tom Terrific* (1957–59). Even Disney got on board with such stylized special projects as *Melody* (1953), the Oscar-winning *Toot, Whistle, Plunk and Boom* (1953) and *Pigs Is Pigs* (1954).

### Award Winning

The Magoo series won two Academy Awards: *When Magoo Flew* (1954) and *Mr Magoo's Puddle Jumper* (1956). Magoo's success paved the way for other progressive cartoons, notably *Gerald McBoing-Boing* (1951). The first McBoing-Boing film, based on a story by Theodore Geisel (Dr Seuss), about a boy who can speak only in sound effects, also went on to win an Oscar. The studio did not just rely solely on these popular characters, however. One-off films such as John Hubley's *Rooty Toot Toot* (1952), a stylized retelling of the Frankie and Johnnie blues saga; Edgar Allan Poe's psychological thriller *The Tell Tale Heart* (1953); and the delightful James Thurber-inspired *Unicorn in the Garden* (1953) all added to the studio's reputation as an influential trendsetter and a force to be reckoned with.

### Troubled Times

In 1952, at the height of the Red Scare and the McCarthy hearings, UPA again became a target. This time John Hubley, perhaps the major creative force at the studio, was blacklisted. Along with Phil Eastman, Hubley left to avoid bringing unwanted governmental scrutiny onto the studio. With Hubley went a good deal of the vision the studio needed to maintain their originality. Other members of the crew, such as Bill Scott, Bobe Cannon, Abe Levitow, Jules Engel, Bill Melendez and Bill Hurtz, tried to keep the

Gerald McBoing-Boing

*Gerald McBoing-Boing* saw UPA make further of use non-realistic animation. They won an Oscar for it, and it provided the impetus for limited animation to be accepted at the major Hollywood cartoon studios, including Warner Bros. and MGM.

The Tell Tale Heart – producer and director

Based on an Edgar Allan Poe story,this limited animation cartoon relied more upon suspension of belief than on realistic depiction of events, and the animators used artistic styles that were not bound to the limitations of the real world to achieve this goal. Pictured are producer Steve Bosustow (left) and director Ted Parmelee.

© UPA Productions/Columbia Pictures

© UPA Productions/Columbia Pictures

© UPA Productions/Columbia Pictures

## 1001 Arabian Nights

This was UPA's first full-length feature, and during production Magoo's chief animator, Pete Burness, left the studio. Although the final result lacked the charm of the Magoo shorts, the design and color were very stylized, reflecting the studio's influential animation techniques.

## Mr Magoo

In Magoo's earliest cartoons, he is like a grizzled, old man; by 1952 his appearance had become rounder and cuter; in 1954 he was stubbier and shorter; and by 1955 he had become what he is like today.

momentum going, and the studio did manage to continue making some terrific films. However, a failed first feature, *1001 Arabian Nights* (1959), diminishing budgets and attrition in the creative ranks took a heavy toll. Soon, Steve Bosustow was the only one left of the original crew. He sold UPA to Henry Saperstein in 1960.

### Moving to TV

Saperstein wanted to expand the studio's product base and began focusing on television. UPA had done one television project, *The Gerald McBoing-Boing Show* (1956–58), which was not a success. But now limited animation, the studio's stylistic calling card, was used to cut costs rather than as a tool for artistic expression. Under Saperstein, two Mr Magoo television series were produced, as well as a Dick Tracy show, but they all suffered either from artistic or creative shortcomings. The one bright spot was the pilot for the otherwise offbeat *The Famous Adventures of Mr Magoo*.

Magoo's *Christmas Carol* (1962) was a wonderful project in all aspects. A musical adaptation of the Charles Dickens tale with songs by Jule Stein, this episode remains a classic piece of work. The rest of the series was forgettable at best – as was almost everything else produced by UPA during this period. A final feature, *Gay Purr-ee*, released by Warner Bros. in 1962, stumbled at the box office and, to all intents and purposes, was the death knell for UPA as an animation studio.

### Heyday Is Over

UPA still existed as an entity, and later Saperstein contracted with DePatie-Freleng for additional Magoo television properties. It also became the distribution arm for a number of Japan's Toho Studios "giant monster" films, including many Godzilla titles. UPA still holds the rights to its library of animated films and characters, but the days of the original studio vision and the unbridled, idealistic creativity that UPA happily brought to the public and the animation industry, while still influential, are long gone.

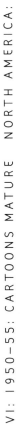

VI: 1950–55: CARTOONS MATURE   NORTH AMERICA: UPA

© UPA Productions/Columbia Pictures

When Disney released *Bambi* in 1942, few would have guessed that it would be the studio's last true feature-length cartoon for eight years. But the demands of World War Two – and then post-war economic doldrums – prevented the company from tackling another one. The drought was finally broken by *Cinderella* in 1950, followed quickly by *Alice in Wonderland* (1951) and *Peter Pan* (1953).

### The Nine Old Men

But much had changed since the *Snow White* era. The Disney-trained artists who would be known as "The Nine Old Men" were starting to dominate animation; star animators of the earlier features were gone from the studio (Art Babbitt, Bill Tytla) or relegated to lesser contributions (Norm Ferguson, Fred Moore). And Walt Disney himself was increasingly preoccupied with other pursuits, from live-action movie-making to the creation of Disneyland.

The conservative products of a conservative time, *Cinderella*, *Alice* and *Peter* – all of which were directed by Clyde Geronimi (1901–89), Wilfred Jackson (1906–88) and Hamilton Luske (1903–68) – do not rival the innovation and depth of the early features. But to give these movies their due, they are polished, tuneful entertainments that remain popular five decades later.

### Return of the Princess

Each of Disney's first five animated features was distinctly different in story, setting and approach. The sixth, *Cinderella*, intentionally returned to *Snow White*'s world of fairy-tale princesses and storybook endings. Disney had seen animation potential in Charles Perrault's 1697 tale of the servant girl and the glass slipper as early as 1922, when he adapted the story into his final *Laugh-O-Gram* short.

By the late 1930s, inspirational artist Bianca Majolie was doing early sketches for a *Cinderella* feature. When Disney resumed feature production in 1947, the story was the first to enter production, apparently at Roy Disney's behest, as Walt preferred *Alice in Wonderland*. Still strapped for cash, the studio

### At The Ball

Disney was determined that *Cinderella* would be a success, and was involved in all aspects of its creation, attending story meetings and commenting on how to improve small details that would add polish to the film.

© The Walt Disney Company

shot a bare-bones live-action version of the movie. The animators, including Marc Davis (1913–2000), Milt Kahl (1909–87) and Eric Larson (1905–88), who were responsible for Cinderella, used photostats of this footage to help plan their drawings. That shortcut led to work that sometimes felt stagier and less soulful than earlier Disney animation had, but the technique was repeated for *Alice* and *Peter Pan*.

## True Cartoon Moments

Ward Kimball (1914–2002) was fortunate enough to get a truly animated assignment: the chase scenes involving Cinderella's mouse friends, Gus and Jacques, and the greedy cat Lucifer. While these sequences were hardly central to the story, they were some of the most confident visual comedy in any Disney feature. Michael Barrier has described them as being "like brilliant short cartoons inserted into this live-action film".

Early Disney soundtracks relied on a mix of character actors, newcomers and homegrown talent. *Cinderella* was dominated by radio veterans, including Ilene Woods (b. 1929) as Cinderella, Eleanor Audley (1905–91) as the stepmother, Verna Felton (1890–1966) as the fairy godmother and Luis Van Rooten (1906–73) as both the king and the grand duke. The songs, by Mack David, Jerry Livingston and Al Hoffman, included such Disney standards-to-be as "A Dream Is a Wish Your Heart Makes" and the Oscar-nominated "Bibbidi-Bobbidi-Boo".

Critics and film-goers in 1950 seemed content to embrace *Cinderella* for what it was: an entertaining return to pleasantly familiar Disney territory. On those terms, it still holds its own today.

© The Walt Disney Company

### Cinderella

Because of the cost of animating a feature-length cartoon, Disney wanted to ensure that all of the scenes that involved humans would work, before they were transferred to cel so live actors were photographed performing some of the key scenes. Some of this footage was traced – the animators were not so keen on this process, as they felt it detracted from their ability to develop characters.

### Gus and Jacques

Rather than be incidental to the action, as in other Disney features, the animals played key roles. Supervising animator Ward Kimball was largely responsible for the creation of the two main mice, Jacques and Gus, and it is rumored that Lucifer (the cat) was modeled on his pet.

© The Walt Disney Company

# ALICE & PETER PAN

Deeply original and quirky, Lewis Carroll's *Alice's Adventures in Wonderland* (1865) seems to defy satisfying adaptation. But that has never stopped movie-makers from trying. At least half-a-dozen film versions preceded the Disney film; Walt Disney's first nod to the British classic had come in 1923 with *Alice's Wonderland*, the first of his *Alice Comedies* about a real girl in an animated world.

### Disney's Brave New World

Sporadic work on Disney's *Alice* feature began as early as 1939—40, when British illustrator David Hall (1905—64) turned out approximately 400 striking, inspirational drawings. Then in 1945, Disney hired *Brave New World* author Aldous Huxley (1894—1963) to work on a story for a live-action/animated version.

When the film finally arrived in 1951 – drawing material from both *Alice* and its sequel, *Through the Looking Glass* – it owed little to Hall's or Huxley's visions. It also bore scant resemblance to John Tenniel's original illustrations. Rather, it was dominated by the brashly American, unapologetically cartoony style of animator Ward Kimball's work. In fact, Kimball was responsible for some of the most memorable moments: the Mad Tea Party scene and the appearances of the Cheshire Cat and Tweedledum and Tweedledee. Also influential was designer Mary Blair (1911—78), whose love of vivid colors and flat shapes helped determine the film's look.

### Disney Down the Rabbit Hole

Like most adapters of *Alice*, Disney gave in to the temptation to cast well-known performers: radio comedians Ed Wynn (1886—1966) and Jerry Colonna (1904—86) played the Mad Hatter and the March Hare. Alice herself was a British girl, Kathryn Beaumont (b. 1938); she promoted the film by appearing in *One Hour in Wonderland*, the first Disney TV special in the 1950s.

Ultimately, Disney's *Alice* retained Carroll's episodic structure but little of his verbal ingenuity. The movie compensated to some degree with its own visual inventiveness, but offered almost no depth of character or story. Neither the press nor movie-goers gave it a warm welcome, and even Disney's own artists seemed eager to disown it: "Alice herself gave us nothing to work with," complained Marc Davis, quoted in Bob Thomas's *Disney's Art of Animation* (1991). Only upon re-release, to theatres and on video, has Alice's reputation modestly improved.

### Peter Pan

Unique among Disney animated features, *Peter Pan* was based on a play: the 1904 British classic by J.M. Barrie (1860—1937), which Barrie turned into the

**Alice**

Disney always had a strong interest in Lewis Carroll's *Alice* books. Sir John Tenniel's original illustraions were freely adapted by Disney's animation team. Months of rough sketches preceded the final model sheets.

© The Walt Disney Company

novel *Peter and Wendy* in 1911. In 1939 Disney obtained film rights to the tale of the boy who would not grow up. On the stage, Peter is typically played by a woman and Tinker Bell is portrayed by a silent beam of light; the audience is encouraged to revive Tink by applauding during the play's climax. Disney abandoned most of these customs. For instance, he found his Peter Pan in studio child star Bobby Driscoll (1937–68), whose most recent role had been Jim Hawkins in *Treasure Island* (1950).

Tinker Bell became a tiny, but shapely, humanized character. She remained speechless, but Marc Davis's superlative animation made the petulant fairy an endlessly expressive character. Disney cast Hans Conried (1917–82) as both Captain Hook and the Darling children's father, following another stage tradition.

## Bringing Peter to Life

In many other ways, the studio put its own imprint on the story. Kathryn Beaumont, who had played Alice, returned as the prim but courageous Wendy, and her brother John was voiced by British actor Paul Collins. But most major vocal characterizations were American, although Conried's foppish Hook at least sounded British, more or less.

Hook's genially dim-witted sidekick Mr Smee sounded like Tex Avery's Droopy – perhaps because he was voiced by the same actor, Bill Thompson (1913–71). Conried and Thompson gave bravura comic performances, and the accompanying animation, by artists such as Frank Thomas and Wolfgang Reitherman (Hook) and Oliver Johnston (Smee) was highly refined slapstick. Some of the Smee footage was by one-time Disney great Fred Moore, in one of his final assignments; he died aged 41 after an accident in November 1952, less than three months before *Pan*'s release.

## Comedy Genius

The heavy dose of pratfall comedy had a profound effect. Unlike earlier Disney villains such as *Snow White*'s Queen or *Pinocchio*'s Stromboli, Hook is hard to take seriously as a threat. That and other elements of the film – flirty mermaids, wacky Indians, cheery songs – made this movie into a light-hearted, somewhat superficial romp. But what a well-executed romp it is. When Peter, Tinker Bell and the Darling children soar over Edwardian London to Sammy Cahn and Sammy Fain's "You Can Fly, You Can Fly", *Peter Pan* is post-war Disney animation at its best.

© The Walt Disney Company

© The Walt Disney Company

**Peter Pan**

As in previous animated Disney films, actors performed the whole production in live-action so that the animators could capture their actions, movements, poses and facial expressions on paper. The actors used props and were properly dressed in costumes.

**Wendy and Tinker Bell**

In the original play, Tinker Bell was never shown except as a projected beam of light. Marc Davis created the feminine pixie seen in the Disney version, her shapely form originating from the "pin-up girls" of World War Two.

*The Little Mermaid* » 276

# WIDESCREEN & 3D

One thing television could not offer home viewers of the early 1950s was a gigantic, panoramic visual experience. Thus, out of competition for audiences, was born Cinemascope. Although the theater owners, and audiences, may have loved the new widescreen format, it did present some new challenges to animated film producers.

## Cinemascope

Gene Deitch was hired as the creative head of Terrytoons when the Columbia Broadcasting System bought the venerable animation studio in 1957. "We had a release schedule of 12 animated films a year – all to be made in Cinemascope," Deitch said. "Now 'Cinemascope' sounds great, but for animation production it was terrible! And our films had to be widescreen because our distributor, Twentieth Century Fox, owned Cinemascope." One problem that he found artistically vexing was the inability to use camera tilts. "Think of it. You tilt the camera just a little in Cinemascope and you start to see the edge of the paper." Another creative limitation was brought on by the fact that CBS, being the owners of a major American television network, naturally wanted their cartoons designed for ultimate broadcast use. "So all the main action had to occur in the middle section of the screen," recalls Deitch. Despite the obstacles, Deitch managed to do an impressive job of Cinemascope layout and design on films such as *The Juggler of Our Lady* (1957), based on the R. O. Blechman book.

Walt Disney Productions faced the aspect ratio problem by shooting their first Cinemascope feature, *Lady and the Tramp* (1955), twice; once for Cinemascope, and once, with altered layouts, for standard screen dimensions. The studio's Donald Duck visited a widescreen Grand Canyon in 1954's *Grand Canyonscope* (wherein Ranger Woodlore advises a crowd to "Spread out, folks. This is Cinemascope!"), while the Disney Oscar-winning short *Toot, Whistle, Plunk and Boom* remains a tour de force in Cinemascope design. Not to be outdone, MGM provided its stars Tom and Jerry, Spike and Tyke and Droopy with widescreen backdrops for nearly 30 cartoons.

© The Walt Disney Company

**Lady and the Tramp**

It took over four years and 200,000 individual drawings to create this feature. Cinemascope, with its superior storytelling potential and dramatic widescreen effects, sometimes quadrupled the work on each scene and increased the overall expense by about 30 per cent.

© The Walt Disney Company

© Famous Studios/Paramount

## 3D Animation Pioneers

Much has been made in recent years of "3D animation", in which the term has incorrectly been used to describe computer-generated (CG) animation, which aims for a naturalistic dimensional representation of images. But "real 3D" animated films go back to the very first presentation to mass audiences of a film using polarizing 3D glasses (the colorless lenses – not the inferior red and green lenses). The ground-breaking film was called *Motor Rhythm* (1939). It featured stop-motion animation with a synchronized score and was shown at the 1939 New York World's Fair. It may have helped inspire the 1950s 3D craze; four short 3D films, two of them animated, were produced for the Festival of Britain in 1951. When the subsequent Hollywood-made 3D feature *Bwana Devil* opened to a big box office in late 1952, the movie business went mad for 3D.

### Popeye

*The Ace of Space* was the only 3D Popeye cartoon that was made, and was dubbed "a stereotoon". Casper the Ghost, Woody Woodpecker and Bugs Bunny also appeared in 3D during this era.

### Toot, Whistle, Plunk and Boom

Pictured is a character from this Oscar-winning short.

© The Walt Disney Company

### Toot, Whistle, Plunk and Boom

This was Disney's first cartoon filmed in Cinemascope. This new technique allowed the characters to move about in a larger proscenium, and gave the animators more opportunity for visual development.

## Crazy for It

From early 1953 through the first six months or so of 1954, American audiences could go to their neighborhood theaters, don a pair of glasses with polarizing lenses and watch their favorite stars in what actually appeared to be three dimensions.

Audiences enjoying watching Edward G. Robinson and John Forsythe vie for the attentions of Kathleen Hughes in Universal's 3D feature *The Glass Web* (1953) might also discover Woody Woodpecker and Buzz Buzzard cavorting on skyscrapers in *Hypnotic Hick* (1953). Crowds flocking to see comedy team Dean Martin and Jerry Lewis tangle with Pat Crowley and Richard Haydn in Paramount's 3D flick *Money from Home* (1953) might also encounter a friendly ghost named Casper starring in the outer space 3D cartoon *Boo Moon* (1954) or the spinach-eating sailor in *Popeye, The Ace of Space* (1953). The RKO 3D release *Dangerous Mission* (1954), starring Victor Mature, Piper Laurie and Vincent Price might also offer its audience the Walt Disney 3D short *Working for Peanuts* (1953), featuring the somewhat less intense trio of Donald Duck and Chip and Dale.

But the 3D craze ran its course. An occasional animated 3D cartoon may be announced nowadays, but the films, few and far between, are usually made for specialized venues. The 2003 feature *Spy Kids 3D* featured up-to-date computer animation, but used the inferior red and green lenses. However, for one shining moment in the 1950s, all Hollywood – and Cartoonland – was in 3D.

# CHUCK JONES IN HIS PRIME

Charles M. "Chuck" Jones grew up in a family where attention to literature and a freewheeling appreciation for any kind of creative expression were evident. While Jones's mother probably had more impact on his artistic sensibilities, it was, in fact, his father who pulled him out of high school in his junior year and sent him to Chouinard Art Institute (now CalArts), to avail himself of a "marketable skill".

## From the Bottom to the Top

During the Great Depression, Jones managed to find work at a string of animation studios, starting at the bottom and working his way up to assistant animator by the time he had signed with the Schlesinger unit in 1936. There he watched and learned from the most creative animation directors of the era: Tex Avery, Bob Clampett, Frank Tashlin and Friz Freleng. In 1938, Chuck was assigned to direct his first cartoon, *The Night Watchman*.

Jones' early films were mostly sentimental, rather "Disneyfied" creations: nicely animated, but with little of the snap or wit that would become his trademark. Films like *The Curious Puppy* (1939), *Bedtime for Sniffles* (1940) or *The Brave Little Bat* (1941) were always clever, but rarely seemed spontaneous or much different from what many other animation directors were doing. Then, in 1942, he directed the almost experimental *The Dover Boys*. Jones admitted that this film, with its lively blend of animation and satiric style, became a benchmark for him – a departure from his storytelling approach, both graphically and narratively. It is possible that Jones's raucous work on the Private Snafu series (1942–45), made for the army during World War Two, may have had some effect on his style as well.

## Developing Personalities

Jones had worked with the Warner Bros. stock characters – Bugs Bunny, Daffy Duck, Porky Pig and Elmer Fudd – from the start, but now he was beginning to codify their personalities, bringing them into sharp relief and contrasting one against the other. Their personalities began to run deeper than just a wise guy, hyperactive wacko or comic foil. Over the next few years, we would come to recognize in Jones's cartoons a deeper psychology and motivation for all of these personalities, except perhaps for Elmer, who remained a doofus throughout. The cartoons became more brisk and willing to let the audience draw its own inferences from an increasingly clever emphasis on character and

### Bully for Bugs

Chuck Jones employed slapstick comedy and timing to an ever-precise degree in his animation. His experiments, at first unpopular with management, later became legendary. *Bully for Bugs* was created immediately after he had been forbidden to make a cartoon about bullfighting.

### Pepé le Pew

Pepé le Pew was a malodorous, amorous skunk, whose object of affection was Penelope the cat. Pepé is said to be a parody of Pepé le Moko, the character played by the legendary actor Charles Boyer in the 1937 movie *Algiers*.

Avery, Jones and Clampett » 86  Freleng and Tashlin » 88

"PEPÉ LE PEW"
© 1960  WARNER BROS. PICTURES INC.

expression. Two cartoons from 1944, *Tom Turk and Daffy* and *Bugs Bunny and the Three Bears* are good examples of this developing style.

Soon Jones would add more characters to the Warner stable. In 1945, he unleashed Pepé le Pew, a skunk with an insatiable romantic streak in *Odor-able Kitty*. He paired Hubie and Bertie and the neurotic Claude Cat in *Mouse Wreckers* in 1948, and Bugs went in for opera in *Long Haired Hare* in 1949. That was the same year that Jones and his longtime writer Michael Maltese came up with *Fast and Furry-ous*, the first in an ever-escalating series of hysterically plotted commentaries on the nature of fanaticism, featuring the hapless Wile E. Coyote and his nemesis, Roadrunner.

## Golden Era

The 1950s were undoubtedly the banner years for Jones. His characters were fully realized, his humor was fearless and his team had worked so long and well together that they could very nearly finish each other's sentences. These were the years of *The Scarlet Pumpernickel* (1950), *The Rabbit of Seville* (1950), *Rabbit Seasoning* (1952), the nearly perfect cartoon about cartoons *Duck Amuck* (1953), and perhaps Jones's crowning achievement of the era, *What's Opera, Doc?* (1957).

© Warner Bros.

### Duck Dodgers

*Duck Dodgers in the 24 1/2th Century* was a spoof of the popular *Buck Rogers in the 25th Century AD* pulp fiction. The cartoon includes highly stylized backgrounds, one of creator Jones's and creator Maurice Noble's trademarks.

There were many other wonderful films of the period. Jones would be nominated for three Academy Awards – *The High Note* in 1960, *Beep Prepared* a year later and *Now Hear This* in 1963. He won an Oscar in 1965 for *The Dot and the Line*, ironically not for Warner Bros., but for MGM. Jones would also become successful in making animated films for television, especially his adaptation of Dr Seuss's *How the Grinch Stole Christmas* (1966) and a terrific series of Rudyard Kipling stories. But is was those years from the mid-1940s through to the late-1950s that seemed to be the real golden age for Chuck Jones: a time for fully realized characters in ideally told tales so brief and ingenious in their structure it could take the breath away, and yet so disarmingly simple that even adults could understand them.

© Warner Bros.

### One Froggy Evening

Only one six-minute cartoon was ever made featuring Michigan J. Frog. The cartoon, complete with spectacular song-and-dance routines, was written by Michael Maltese, and the frog went on to become Warner Bros. TV network's official logo in the 1990s.

In any career there is usually one major defining moment. For Ray Harryhausen (b. 1920), it came at the impressionable age of 13 when he walked into Grauman's Chinese Theater in Hollywood to see some "ape picture" he knew little about. That movie was the 1933 smash-hit *King Kong* and it would set Harryhausen on the path to becoming the "father of modern visual effects".

## Monster Influence

If Harryhausen is the patriarch of stop-motion-effects animation, then the title of grandfather most certainly goes to Willis O'Brien, the man who breathed life into the great Kong and the other prehistoric inhabitants of Skull Island. Years earlier, O'Brien had astonished audiences with the dinosaur animation he performed for the 1925 screen adaptation of Sir Arthur Conan Doyle's *The Lost World* (1912). But it was *King Kong* that fueled young Harryhausen's insatiable thirst for knowledge about the process that allowed human actors to share the screen with towering monsters from another time.

### The Golden Voyage of Sinbad

This is the second film in the Sinbad trilogy from 1974. The others were *The Seventh Voyage of Sinbad* (1958) and *Sinbad and the Eye of the Tiger* (1977).

© Warner Bros.

## Early Lessons

Harryhausen was lucky to have parents who not only encouraged his creative pursuits, but also contributed to his projects. His father was a machinist and constructed the metal ball-and-socket armatures for his puppets, while his mother sewed the costumes. She even let Ray cut up her fur coat to cover his first stop-motion model, a man-eating cave bear. Throughout his high-school years, Harryhausen continued to experiment, and he was eventually granted the opportunity to show some of his puppets to his idol, O'Brien. O'Brien was impressed, but told the budding animator that his stegosaurus's legs looked like sausages and suggested he take anatomy and art courses. This advice would prove invaluable to Harryhausen and his ability to push the lifelike qualities of his creations.

At the age of 18, Harryhausen landed his first professional job, working on the *Puppetoons* shorts George Pal was producing for Paramount. His two-year tenure there ended when Pearl Harbor was bombed and he enlisted in the army, where his stop-motion training film *How to Bridge a Gorge* got him assigned to Colonel Frank Capra's Special Service Division.

### The Valley of Gwangi

*Gwangi* was a pet project of Harryhausen's since the 1940s. His Dynamation technique allowed a stop-motion model to be animated directly in front of a screen showing live-action footage with human actors.

George Pal and Puppetoons » 92 *Jurassic Park* » 306

© Warner Bros.

## Forging His Style

Returning from the war with a load of discarded 16 mm Kodachrome film, Harryhausen began producing a series of fairy tales for children. Combining his own style with what he learned from working with Pal, he animated the fables using articulated models with a series of replaceable heads. The last of the shorts, *The Tortoise and the Hare*, had just gone into production when he was called by O'Brien to serve as lead animator on the 1949 feature *Mighty Joe Young*. The opportunity would lead to a long and lucrative career creating awe-inspiring visual effects for such indelible classics as *The Beast From 20,000 Fathoms* (1953), *It Came From Beneath the Sea* (1955), *20 Million Miles to Earth* (1957), *The Seventh Voyage of Sinbad* (1958), *Jason and the Argonauts* (1963) and *The Valley of Gwangi* (1969).

While Mighty Joe Young was another giant ape picture produced to capitalize on the popularity of King Kong, the differences in the animation are striking. Harryhausen was already showing that he was improving the art form O'Brien originated. While O'Brien masterfully infused Kong with personality, he often applied broad strokes in his increments, which lent a degree of jerkiness to the animation and made the great ape move a bit too fast on-screen. Harryhausen handled Joe with more subtlety, and slowed the animation down to convey a sense of scale and help make the small model appear huge to audiences.

**The Valley of Gwangi – sketch**

Before starting work on a film, Harryhausen would draw in charcoal the most exciting scenes he wanted to do. From the drawings came 300 to 400 pen-and-ink sketches used to flesh out the sequences, so as to clarify the action during filming.

## Dynamation

Harryhausen's signature innovation is something he dubbed "Dynamation". The process involved elaborate setups that sandwiched the stop-motion animation models between glass matte paintings or optically matted foreground elements and rear-screen-projected background plates. The effect produced more convincing composites as giant monsters rampaged through city streets and humans battled sword-wielding skeletons.

Having witnessed the birth of a new era in special effects with the arrival of *Star Wars* (1977), Harryhausen put his surface gauges away after finishing the 1981 *Clash of the Titans*. He briefly came out of retirement in 2002 to help animators Mark Caballero and Seamus Walsh complete *The Tortoise and the Hare*, the short he had abandoned 50 years earlier. A year later he received his long-deserved star on the Hollywood Walk of Fame, yet another testament to his enduring influence on the motion-picture industry and the impact his films will continue to have on generations of creature-feature fans.

© Warner Bros.

Aardman Animation » 322   CGI Victorious » 338

With the Red Scare of the late 1940s, the Canadian government began cleaning its house of "Communist sympathizers" working within the public sector. Several artists at the National Film Board (NFB) suspected of having ties to Communism were asked to leave. Norman McLaren, a one-time member of the Communist Party, was spared. In 1949, Jim McKay, head of the animation unit, wanted a change and left along with George Dunning to set up a commercial studio in Toronto. Colin Low, a man who would later go on to be one of the creators of IMAX, was named department head.

### The Romance of Transportation in Canada

Setting NFB's trademark style, this Oscar-nominated short took a whimsical look at how Canadians solved the problem of covering their country's vast distances with transport options from carts and horses to trains and planes.

© 1952 National Film Board of Canada

### Early Successes

The film board had begun moving beyond the more experimental techniques they had pioneered. Although there were a few earlier attempts, *Teamwork – Past and Present* (1951) is considered the NFB's first traditional cel-animated production. Their second cel-animated film, *The Romance of Transportation in Canada* (1953), not only set the template for the cartoony-style the NFB became known for, but was also nominated for an Academy Award.

Bob Verrall and Wolf Koenig, along with Low, were responsible for *Teamwork* and *Romance of Transportation*. They would be key film-makers in the NFB's development not only in animation, but also as documentarians, directing two of the Film Board's finest documentaries: *City of Gold* (1957) and *Lonely Boy* (1961). Their immense influence is still felt at the NFB today.

### Huff and Puff

Co-directed by Gerald Potterton and Grant Munro, *Huff and Puff* was made for air force crews informing them of the dangers of hyperventilation in high altitudes, and gave advice as to how to recover with appropriate respiration.

© 1955 National Film Board of Canada

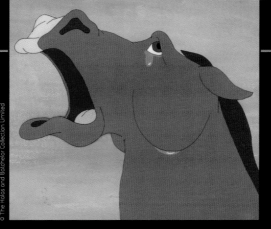

## Boxer

The animals' reaction to their beloved Boxer's fate is typical of this film: resigned stoicism rather than righteous anger. Halas and Batchelor's version of Orwell's novel was not sentimental and was aimed at adults, rather than children.

## Animal Chorus

The animals, having been so badly treated by Famer Jones, join in a barnyard rebellion and run the farm themselves. At first all is well, until some of the pigs begin to assume more of the power.

enough to handle the job; other studios such as Larkins and George Moreno's were decidedly minor in comparison.

This was also a new venture for Halas & Batchelor. Up to then, they had only been producing industrial, promotional and informational shorts for the Ministry of Information, and they were by no means certain that they could produce something that would carry as much dramatic impact as Orwell's tale.

# HALAS & BATCHELOR'S FEATURE

The idea of a feature cartoon that dealt with such a serious subject as anti-Communism and contained little or no laughs was a challenge to the Halas & Batchelor team, but they proceeded and started production in 1951.

## Starting Work

In an interview for *Animator* magazine in 1989, John Halas revealed that the making of *Animal Farm* was not without its problems: "From its commencement it was like travelling down a long dark tunnel with no light at the end, and when at last a faint flicker could be seen, I raced to emerge into the light of a new day." Halas was against taking a strong anti-Stalin stand and insisted that it had to be a universal film for all audiences. His opinions were overruled, resulting in the overlaying theme being one of a specifically adult nature – a fight for freedom. In retrospect, Halas's personal view of the film's basic flaw was that far too much attention had been paid to "unnecessary" details rather than to the overall flow of the film.

## Disneyfication

Ex-Disney animator John Reed was called in to handle the animation direction. Reed had recently been involved with David Hand's GBA studio and was responsible for the "Disney-esque" appearance of *Animal Farm*. In most cases the Disney style jars with the story, seen, for instance, with the annoying intrusion of a "cute" duckling that is constantly pushed aside by its peers. The other main animators involved were Eddie Radage, Arthur Humberstone, Ralph Ayres, Harold Whitaker and Frank Moysey. The final storyboard for 75 minutes of action consisted of fewer than 2,000 sketches used from an original collection of 10,000. The original storyboard followed the novel and included three confrontations between animals and humans but, in film terms, three fights proved too cumbersome and the number was reduced to just two.

While production on *Animal Farm* was forging ahead in London's Soho Square, a second unit was formed at Halas's other studio 120 miles away in Stroud to help carry some of the load. In addition to all this, the studio still carried on with their normal scheduled workload.

## Sound and Music

Hungarian composer Matyas Seiber was brought in to compose the imposing atmospheric music. His greatest musical problem was a "battle hymn" for the animals when about to overthrow Farmer Jones. This had to be written as a parody of all revolutionary music and sung without words by the animals. After singers who could sing in "animal" tones had been found, the final mixing of music and animals amounted to as many as eight separate recording tracks.

**Storyboard**

The bleak atmosphere portrayed in the film suits the subject-matter. The backgrounds are darkly colored and broadly textured, with smoothly illustrated figures shrugging off the yoke of oppression.

**Pigs —sketches**

The pigs in Orwell's allegory, and Halas and Batchelor's adaptation, were direct counterparts of figures in the Russian Revolution: Old Major is Karl Marx; Napoleon is Joseph Stalin; and Snowball is Lenin and Trotsky.

© Jacques Prévert / Paul Grimault

### Roi et l'Oiseau

When restoring and completing the film, Grimault retained the look and feel of the original. Although released in 1980, the film has the authentic look of a late-1940s animated feature, which is when work began on the original, *Le Bergère et la Ramoneur*.

### Roi et l'Oiseau – sketch

The film was a labor of love, and includes beautifully designed sets and backgrounds, caverns, towers, arches, Venetian canals and squares, and vast palaces with Escher-like staircases. Each of the animators worked on their own characters, giving each their own personality and characteristics.

© Jacques Prévert / Paul Grimault

reception by the critics. This version incensed Paul Grimault and Jacques Prévert enough to bring court actions against Sarrut and have their names removed from the credits.

## The Metamorphosis of Mr Wonderbird

*Mr Wonderbird* had been a bone of contention with Grimault since his ousting in 1950. Then, in 1967, he managed to acquire the rights to it along with control over all of the negative stock. With help from Jacques Prévert, Grimault hoped to put matters right by reconstructing the film in a different way. They managed to round up the surviving animators who had worked on the original, as well as many new artists and the one surviving actor of the initial French voice cast, Roger Blin. Work began on re-creating the whole project.

As no original artwork remained, the artists had to retain the original hand-drawn 1940s style to match the remaining animation on-screen. This was certainly a laborious task, as styles had moved on since 1947 and the artists only had the film as a reference.

Production was finally completed by 1980, this time titled *Le Roi et l'Oiseau* ('The King and the Mockingbird'), and an English-language version was dubbed using American actors. It now stands, 33 years after the original concept, as a monument to Jacques Prévert, who sadly died three years before completion and was never able to see his labor of love in its final form.

A

Surrealist in conception and tragicomic in tone, Lenica's films often represent states of mind and the urban experience. This was made in 1964, a time when Polish artists would cloak their indictments of Stalinism, power politics and repression in allegorical storytelling and ironical wit.

**Labyrinth**

This is a self-consciously Kafka-esque tale of a winged lonely man literally devoured by totalitarian rule, and is considered to be one of the finest political animations ever made.

started in the 1950s, and Lingurski made his first film, *The Terrible Bomb* in 1951. These early films are important in that they established roots for future Bulgarian animators, but due to poor funding and inexperience, many of these early films are technically crude.

Things begin to brighten in 1955 with the emergence of Todor Dinov. Dinov, considered the father of Bulgarian animation, had studied under legendary Russian animator Ivan Ivanov-Vano. He became an important teacher and promoter of Bulgarian animation and earned acclaim for his first film, *Marko the Hero* (1955).

Jarava's animation career was short-lived, however. Because of conflicts with management, who favored USSR or Czechoslovakian-trained animators over the self-educated Jarava, he was forced to resign.

## Poland

Aside from Wladyslav Starewicz, a handful of men – including Franziska and Stefan Thermerson, who made experimental collages including the brilliant *Europe* (1931–32) – tried their hand at animation in Poland from 1917–39. However, Polish animation as an organized entity did not begin until after World War Two.

Following the war, the new Communist regime in Poland invested heavily in cinema. Animation, however, was not taken so seriously. Despite this, Zenon Wasilewski, a prominent pre-war animator, was intent on finishing a film he had shot in 1939. To do this he moved to Lodz, where he started a production and distribution company, which later became the famous puppet studio Semafor. A drawn animation studio was also established in Katowice in 1947. During this time the Polish Communists kept animation, like all of Polish cinema, on a short leash. Following the Soviet model, animation was dominated by propaganda and folk tales, espousing the concept "national in form – socialist in content". Nevertheless, a structure was in place that provided training for future Polish animators like Witold Giersz, who would make his debut in 1956 with *The Mystery of the Old Castle*, followed by what many consider his finest film, *Little Western* (1960).

## Sparks of Creativiy

The most notable productions from this period come from Wlodimierz Haupe and Halina Bielinska. In 1954, the duo made the first Polish animated feature, a puppet film called *Janosik*. They followed this with an innovative film created with matchboxes called *Changing of the Guard* (1959), which won the Golden Palm at the Cannes Film Festival.

In 1955, an event took place that would drastically change the direction of Polish animation: the Arsenal Art Exhibition held in Warsaw. The exhibition featured an array of Polish fine arts, all of them very different from the prescribed "social realism". The exhibition stimulated two young artists in particular, Jan Lenica (b. 1928) and Walerian Borowczyk (b. 1923), who, a year later, would translate what they saw to animation.

The first half of the 1950s was the eve of the establishment of Japan's professional animation industry. Theatrical animated shorts started out in black and white, but they looked more like the competing modern American color cartoons in art style and quality of motion — Iwao Roda's *The Forest Concert* (1953), for instance, seems to show a Tex Avery influence. They also averaged twice as long as the six- to eight-minute American shorts.

## Changing to Color

Notable titles of this period include *The Gnome and the Green Caterpillar* by Hideo Furasawa (1950), *The Ant and the Pigeon* by Hajime Yuhara (1953), *Story of the Little Rabbit* (1954) written by Taiji Yabushita and directed by Yasuji Mori, *Kawataro the Kappa* (1954) by Taiji Yabushita, and in 1955 came Japan's first color theatrical releases, *The Happy Violin* by Taiji Yabushita and *Onbu, the Little Goblin* by Ryuichi Yokoyama. Nihon Doga, with Sanae Yamamoto as president/executive producer, remained the largest studio, producing one or two films per year.

## Fine-Art Animation

This was also the beginning of the division between popular animation made for commercial theatrical or TV release, and more artistic animation made for international film festivals. Noburo Ofuji became the first Japanese animator to gain international acclaim when his *The Great Buddha* (1951) and *The Whale* (1952) were shown at the 1952 and 1953 Cannes Film Festivals, and his 1955 *The Ghost Ship* at the 1956 Venice Film Festival.

*The Whale*, a remake of his 1927 cut-paper film, substituting colored translucent cellophane for the solid-black silhouettes, was praised by Pablo Picasso. This prestige was recognized in Japan in 1963 when the annual Mainichi Film Festival created the Noburo Ofuji Award for innovative excellence in animation. Its first winner was Osamu Tezuka for his *Stories on a Street Corner* (1962). In 1953 Tadahito Mochinaga returned from China to Japan, where he soon put his experience with Chinese-style stop-motion animation to use in both fine-art and commercial puppet animation.

© Tezuka Productions Co. Ltd

### Aladdin and a Magic Lamp

Tadahito Mochinaga, who together with Kihachiro Kawamoto produced this 1953 puppet animation, holds a unique position in the history of both Japanese and Chinese animated films. He was the first animator to use the multi-plane camera in Japan, and he also made the first stop-motion puppet animations in China and Japan. Mochinaga was among the founding members who built the Shanghai Animation Film Studio.

### Stories on a Street Corner

Although Osamu Tezuka is internationally renowned for his manga, such as Astro Boy, his experimental animation should not be forgotten. There was a limited budget for stories, and to reduce the number of moving pictures, posters and other non-moving objects were used as characters, which gave an innovative impression.

**Tei Wei**

Pictured here at the 1995 Annecy Animation Festival is the Chinese master animator Tei Wei, with his ASIFA award which was presented to him in recognition of his life's work. He is accompanied by his friend, the Swiss animator Georges Schwizgebel.

## Disney of the East

In March 1951, Toei Company, Ltd. was founded. Within a couple of years, it grew to be one of Japan's largest live-action motion-picture production studios and distributors, with a chain of theatres throughout the nation.

In 1955, one of its executives, Hiroshi Okawa (1896–1971), decided that Toei should add an animation department to make the studio "the Disney of the East". After studying Japan's animation industry and being impressed by Nihon Doga's director Taiji Yabushita and key animator Yasuji Mori, Toei bought the Nihon Doga studio outright.

On 31 July 1956, Nihon Doga metamorphosed into Toei Doga (Toei Animation Co., Ltd.), a subsidiary of Toei Co., with Okawa as its first president. Yamamoto remained as its supervising producer. With Toei's funding, Japan's first major animation studio was born.

## China: The Shanghai Studio

In February 1950, the Chinese government transferred Tong Pei's animation department under director Te Wei and assistant Fang Ming from Changchun in Manchuria to the much larger Shanghai Film Studios. The greater resources and talent pool of artists and ex-animators in cosmopolitan Shanghai ("the Hollywood of China") gradually led to what is referred to as "the first Golden Age of Chinese animation", from around 1956 to the Cultural Revolution in 1965.

Pressed to show what they could do, the expanded animation studio produced the short cartoon animation *Thank You, Kitty*, directed by Fang Ming (Mochinaga), by the end of 1950. The years 1950 to 1955 were a period of setup and experimentation. Foreign animation, particularly that of China's political friend the Soviet Union, was studied.

## Striving for a Distinctive Look

Mochinaga completed the first color animation tests before returning to Japan. Wan Chao-chen returned from America, where he had been studying animation, to direct the puppet animation *The Little Heroes* in 1953; and in 1954 Wan Lai-ming and Gu-chan returned from Hong Kong. Although Chinese cartoons created during this period were made primarily for domestic audiences (especially children) some, including *Why Crows Are Black* and the 1955 *The Magic Paintbrush* by Jin Xi (1919–97), were also designed as art films to be shown at Cannes, Venice and other European film festivals to bring international attention to Chinese animation. But after *Why Crows Are Black* was mistaken at the 1955 Venice Festival for Soviet animation, Te Wei was determined that Chinese animation should have a distinctive Chinese look.

# VII

## 1956–60:
# TO THE TUBE

Television animation adapted to lower budgets, faster schedules and a new medium. Hanna-Barbera lead the way with Huckleberry Hound, Yogi Bear and The Flintstones. TV commercials became a lucrative new industry for animators – with powerful art direction as important as the sponsored message. Theatrical shorts began to peter out, though Disney produced his most expensive production, *Sleeping Beauty*, and UPA created a low budget *Mr Magoo* feature film.

Animation artists emerged outside the US – Zagreb produced the first non-Hollywood cartoon short to win an Oscar, Canadian Richard Williams made his mark in London, Osamu Tezuka tried his hand at animation, and Karel Zamen and Jiri Trinka offered unique stop-motion films from Eastern Europe. This was the time when animation was first seriously considered as a varied art form, and international festivals rose to celebrate the field and the film-makers.

It is television, however, which had the greatest impact at this time, expanding creative possibilities and creating new jobs – but sacrificing certain artistic qualities, and beginning to target children as its core audience.

theatrical animation on television budgets and schedules was virtually impossible.

## Crusader Rabbit

The first to attempt the "impossible" were Alex Anderson, the nephew of Terrytoons' founder Paul Terry, and Jay Ward, a young real-estate man with artistic aspirations. Together they created *Crusader Rabbit*, the first cartoon series made specifically for television, which over the next two years popped up on a handful of NBC affiliates. Sporting animation so rudimentary as to resemble a story reel, the adventures of Crusader and his tiger sidekick Rags (also known as Ragland T. Tiger) were presented in serialized form before leaving the airwaves in 1951. Jay Ward, of course, would be heard from again.

The gimmick of serializing short animated segments would be used by virtually every producer who entered television in the 1950s. It was the format for Terrytoons' *Tom Terrific* (1957), which aired on the daily children's show *Captain Kangaroo*; Cambria Productions' adventure series *Clutch Cargo* (1959), which employed the bizarre and creepy technique of superimposing live-action mouths over drawn faces; Q.T. Hush (1960) a comedy/mystery cartoon with a noirish veneer produced by a company called Animation Associates; and Joe Oriolo's revitalized *Felix the Cat* (1960) from Trans-Lux Productions. But the greatest and most lasting impact on animation would come from another serialized cartoon: Hanna-Barbera's *The Ruff and Reddy Show* (1957).

## Distinguished Reputation

By the mid-1950s, William Hanna and Joseph Barbera were already cartoon royalty. Their Tom and Jerry shorts for MGM had won a record seven Academy Awards out of 13 nominations, most recently for *Johann Mouse* (1953). With the retirement in 1955 of Fred Quimby, the nominal and non-creative corporate head of the MGM animation division, they had become the studio's official producers, with control over every cartoon unit. In 1957, though, MGM decided to shut down its entire cartoon operation, citing high production costs and diminished returns in a changing marketplace as the reasons. Hanna and Barbera were left with few options since the short theatrical cartoon business was in decline throughout Hollywood.

### Colonel Bleep

*Colonel Bleep* was another low-budget, early TV cartoon series. It was the first made-for-TV cartoon produced in color, but as its production values were also not high, it did not stand the test of time and by the late 1960s was rarely seen.

© Soundac Studios

## The Little Island

Richard Williams worked for both Disney and UPA studios, and in 1955 he began work on the 33-minute animated film *The Little Island*, which won the BAFTA Award for Best Animated Film in 1959. This piece gained him immediate recognition as a professional and highly talented animator.

## Truth, Beauty & Good

Richard Williams' ground-breaking, experimental film, completed at TVC studios in the late 1950s, was the result of hours of painstaking work by him and his team of animators.

Having earned enough money to see him through art school, he had enough cash left over to buy a car to transport himself back to the Disney Studios with classmate Carl Bell. However, Williams was quickly to become disenchanted by the whole Disney system.

## The Little Island

Disillusioned by animation in general, next on the agenda was a two-year stopgap in Ibiza; his "beach bum" period where he painted, sunbathed, swam in the ocean and played jazz. It was during this idyllic interlude that the idea of his first film, *The Little Island* (1958), was born.

The changing scene of British television that occurred in the mid-1950s all happened with the coming of commercial TV in 1955. Suddenly London was the place to be, so Dick loaded himself up with an armful of drawings of *The Little Island* and set off, arriving at the door of George Dunning's newly formed TV Cartoons studio. He supplemented the cost of Island by working on commercials for dog food, Guinness and Mother's Pride sliced bread during the day, and his own project by night.

The *Little Island* took three years of late nights and weekends to complete, with assistance from George Dunning, his staff and equipment. Made in color and widescreen Cinemascope, the film presents a parable concerning three characters representing Truth, Beauty and Good who live together on a desert isle — and certainly do not live up to their image. They ultimately exterminate themselves through a war. This half-hour epic was well received by critics and festival-goers, enabling Williams to continue pursuing his dream.

© Richard Williams/TV Cartoons

© Dusan Vukotic, *The Playful Robot*, Zagreb Fil

In 1956, both the national and Croatian governments completely withdrew their financial support of both Duga Film and its short-lived successor, Zora Film. But the animators in the Croatian capital were not to be denied. They now turned to another company, Zagreb Film, which at the time was working exclusively on documentaries. The studio agreed to distribute anything the local animators produced, and they jumped at the opportunity. When Dusan Vukotic's (1927–98) *The Playful Robot* (1956) won an award at the Pula Film Festival on the Istrian peninsula in Croatia, the new Zagreb Film was off and running as an animation studio, soon to be one of the most influential in the world. *The Playful Robot* was directed by Vukotic, who would later win the studio an Oscar. The film also marked the debut of other animators who would go on to have successful careers at the studio. The drawings were by Aleksandar Marks and Boris Kolar, the design by Zlatko Bourek, and the animation by Vladimir Jutrisa.

## The Zagreb School

Unified by a commitment to animation and to giving artists free reign, as well as a distinctive white horse as its new logo, the new studio began producing animation at a rapid clip. Its animation style soon became known as "the Zagreb School". In addition to limiting the number of drawings against rudimentary or abstract backgrounds, in the early days another of the studio's pioneering distinctions was the interchangeability of the artists working on direction, design, drawing and story. Ironically, in just a few years the Zagreb School also became known for the film-makers' propensity towards writing, designing and directing their own films. Somehow the two philosophies were not contradictory, as the most talented artists all worked on each other's films. The result was bold cartoons unified in design, tone and message.

## Critical Success

The new studio had a breakthrough in the spring of 1958 when it began screening some of its films at the Oberhausen Film Festival in Germany. The following year, a program of films from the studio at the Cannes Festival in France received rave reviews from both

### The Playful Robot

*The Playful Robot* was the first animated film to be produced by the new Zagreb film studio. This scene is an example of Dusan Vukotic's fondness for using simple caricature drawings dancing across a neutral background.

### Ersatz

*Ersatz* shows the Zagreb style of reduced animation at its best. The focus on the crucial elements of the graphics, direction, sound, character and movement, as well as the idea and humor, all helped this to be such a critically acclaimed film.

## Panda and the Magic Serpent

This was the first Japanese animated feature film in color. It is based on a Chinese legend and tells the story of Xu-Xian, a young boy who is forced to free his pet snake. The snake is actually a young snake-goddess, Bai-Niang, who searches for and is eventually re-united with Xu-Xian.

## Fukusuke

*Fukusuke*'s creator Ryuichi Yokoyama, has received many awards and honors throughout his career. His hometown Kochi City awarded him as the first "Honored Citizen" in 1996 and has built the Yokoyama Gallery within a new museum, which it is hoped will become a national center for animation.

style. Otogi also produced a short art film, *More Than 50,000*, in 1961 as well as Japan's first animated TV series and several animated TV commercials. Then, without explanation, Otogi disappeared and Yokoyama abandoned animation. After retiring as a cartoonist in the early 1970s, he became a fine-art painter and sculptor, winning many national cultural awards and cartoonist societies' awards into his nineties.

## Puppet Animation

Tadahito Mochinaga's return to Japan in 1953 coincided with the birth of the Japanese TV industry. He was hired to produce two one-minute beer commercials, which he did in stop-motion puppet animation with assistant Kihachiro Kawamoto (b. 1924). In 1955 Mochinaga created the Puppet Animation Film Studio to make films for screening at elementary schools, producing nine from *The Little Devil and Princess Uriko* (1956) to *The Fox Who Became King* (1960). He also took in commercial commissions, using them for experimentation, such as the 1957 beer commercial *Once Upon a Time There Was Beer*, directed by Tadasu Iizawa, which combined puppet animation by Kawamoto with colored cellophane animation by Ofuji.

In 1958, Mochinaga's *Little Black Sambo Conquers the Tigers* (1956) won the Best Film Award in the Films for Children category at the first Vancouver International Film Festival. This led to a contract two years later for Mochinaga to produce stop-motion animation for US television for Arthur Rankin Jr.'s Videocraft International, soon to become Rankin/Bass.

© Toei Doga

# VIII

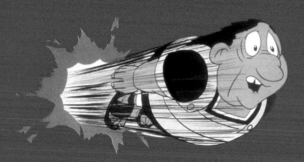

## 1961–70:
# INTERNATIONAL EXPLOSION

By the 1960s, animation production was a global industry — and distinctive artists of all stripes had emerged. There was an explosion of frame-by-frame talent, studios and production. From Zagreb in Yugoslavia and the Pannonia Studio in Hungary, to Bruno Bozetto in Italy and Osamu Tezuka in Japan, they were joined by exciting animated films from China, France and Great Britain.

Britain had the most exciting project in the 1960s, *Yellow Submarine*. With the Beatles' blessing, this animated masterpiece fits into the style of the times — one-part pop art, two-parts psychedelia, with a dash of rock'n'roll. Along with a good story, plenty of gags and cutting-edge art direction, *Yellow Submarine* was a cartoon classic, which proved that an animated feature did not have to be pseudo-Disney.

Walt Disney himself died during this decade, while TV animation grew to new financial heights — and creative depths. *The Flintstones* led to *The Jetsons*, *Jonny Quest*, *Scooby-Doo* and a whole slew of Hanna-Barbarians. Jay Ward brought forth *Rocky & Bullwinkle* and Filmation churned out *The Archies*. The Pink Panther was born — and brought some life to the theatrical short. Underground independent animation grew as movie cameras and film equipment got cheaper and easier to access.

A new generation was beginning.

To some, the television cartoon-factory system established by Hanna-Barbera in the early 1960s signaled the ruination of the American animation industry. The phrase "illustrated radio" was coined by purists to describe it. But strictly from an industry standpoint, without Hanna-Barbera and their ability to keep producing animation at a previously unheard-of level, the American animation business might be very different today. In fact, it might not even exist.

## Animation Takes Over the Airwaves

The immediate success and influence of Hanna-Barbera on television in general can be measured by glancing at the network prime-time television schedule of fall 1961, which contained three hours of animation every week – four hours if *Walt Disney's Wonderful World of Color* (formerly *Disneyland*) aired an animated program on the Sunday. In addition to *The Flintstones* and Hanna-Barbera's *Top Cat* (1961), there was Jay Ward's *The Bullwinkle Show*, a revamping of his ground-breaking *Rocky and his Friends* (1959); *Beany and Cecil* (1960), the signature show of animation's gonzo genius, Bob Clampett; *The Bugs Bunny Show* (1960), which repackaged vintage Warner Bros. cartoons inside new linking footage created by the studio's senior directors, Chuck Jones, Friz Freleng and Robert McKimson; *The Alvin Show* (1961), an animated rendition of the popular "singing chipmunk" novelty records of Ross Bagdasarian; and the forgettable *Calvin and the Colonel* (1961), an animated derivation of the radio chestnut *Amos and Andy*, featuring the original actors Freeman Gosden and Charles Correll.

All this was in addition to the series that sprung up for the syndication market, including Art Clokey's clay-animated *Davey and Goliath* financed by the Lutheran Council of Churches; Terrytoons' cornpone-flavored *Deputy Dawg* (1960); and UPA's rather appalling *The Dick Tracy Show* (1961), in which the square-jawed police detective supervised such jokey, racially insulting assistant detectives as "Jo Jitsu" and "Go Go Gomez". Animation was also creeping into the burgeoning Saturday morning marketplace, with such shows as *King Leonardo and His Short Subjects* (1960), a regal comedy starring a lion king.

### Fred and Wilma

*The Flintstones* was based on the sitcom, *The Honeymooners* which ran during the late 1950s. *The Flintstones'* success saw the release of other prime-time animated shows also based on sitcoms: *Top Cat* was almost identical to *Sgt Bilko*, and *Calvin & the Colonel* was extremely similar to *Amos and Andy*.

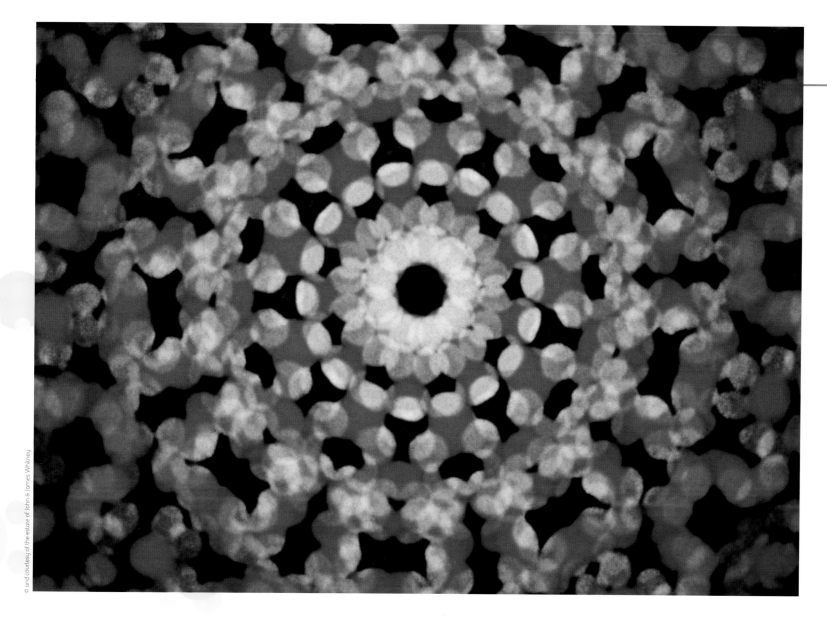

## Lapis

*Lapis* was made with John Whitney's prototype motion-control camera. Motion-control meant that a camera could be programmed to shoot an image over and over with subtle variations. In *Lapis* a configuration of 250 dots, via calibrated camera rotations and color filters, cascade and dance kaleidoscopically.

## Yantra

Painstakingly drawn by hand, this film takes its title from a Sanskrit word for "machine" or prayer wheel, and melds ancient mysticism to the sublime visual effects of ultrasmooth mathematical motion.

works ever made. *Yantra* (1955) is described as a series of "quasi-musical variations of implosions and explosions" and, like his other films, is conceived as a visual/spiritual experience. He returned to painting before finishing *Lapis* (1965), which again used images derived from a series of points; while he did use his brother's computer-guided camera equipment during production, the images themselves were handcrafted.

James's last project, left unfinished when he died, was a tetralogy representing the four primary elements: fire, water, air and earth. The first, *Dwija* (1976) uses images of a bird being reborn, bathed in liquid light, while the climatic image in *Wu Ming* (1977) is of a black circle gradually shrinking until it disappears, creating a feeling of grandiosity. *Kang Jing Xiang* (1982) is perhaps best described by translating the title as "what is seen during a lustrous religious ecstasy", and features contrasts between misty and bright, pulsing images. Unfortunately, James died before completing the last film in the project, but the three that exist offer fascinating viewing.

# YELLOW SUBMARINE

Although not actually the first animated cartoon to jump on the Beatles' bandwagon, *Yellow Submarine* still stands out as a landmark in cult-animation history.

## What's It All About?

The prolog takes place in the mythical region of Pepperland, where everything is tranquil and echoes to the sound of laughter and the music of Sgt Pepper's band. A hostile sneak attack by the music-loathing Blue Meanies leaves the band encased in a bubble and the inhabitants frozen in time. Old Fred is the only one who manages to escape the wrath of the Blue Meanies and goes to find help, making his exit in the very vehicle that had brought their forefathers to Pepperland, a flying yellow submarine. Fred successfully takes the sub to the rain-sodden streets of Liverpool, where he encounters Ringo and begs his assistance. Soon John, George and Paul are rounded up and they set off in the yellow submarine on a journey to Pepperland, a land lying firmly beneath the jackboot of the despotic Blue Meanies.

Finally disembarking at their destination, the foursome prepare for the battle by first freeing the trapped band with a rousing chorus of 'All You Need Is Love', which brings the life back into the populace of Pepperland. This takes the Meanies by surprise and a battle ensues. The outcome has the villains and their cohorts being finally routed and the Chief Meanie's views drastically altered as he realizes that love and music are not really the demons he imagined them to be. With the return of serenity in Pepperland, a celebration in music and song takes place with the Fab Four and their counterparts joining in with 'All Too Much'.

In a filmed epilogue, the Beatles appear and comment on the film. John claims that "newer and bluer Meanies have been sighted" and that the best reply is to go out on a song... 'All Together Now!'

**The Fab Four – heads**

Chief artist Heinz Edelmann brought his unique vision to the pacing of the film to infuse it with a heightened sense of excitement and vibrant immediacy. He thought that the film should be a series of interconnected shorts, as it would keep the interest going until the end. It was an effective approach, and a technique that broadened the visual imagination of animated films.

**The Flower Lovers**

Common to many of Bordo's films is the theme of survival in impossible situations. The protagonist is usually an ordinary person trying to enjoy a life with privacy and respect in a society that is continually harassing her or him, for example surviving in a city gone mad through an obsession with exploding flowers in *The Flower Lovers*.

**The Bird and the Worm**

A scene from Grgic's series for children, one of many that he produced.

slapstick, part philosophy. Some of his later work includes *Learning to Walk* (1978), which tells the story of a man whose countrymen each try to teach him their own style of walking, although he already knows how to walk just fine, and *Exciting Love Story* (1989), in which a man is in search of his sweetheart, Gloria.

## Zlatko Grgic

Another of Zagreb's comic masters was Zlatko Grgic (1931–88), whose debut film in 1965 at the age of 20 was *The Devil's Work*. It demonstrated his comedic talents at their best, as a well-meaning fellow learns to appreciate the benefits of "devilish" behavior. His other films included *Little and Big* (1966), his take on the classic cartoon chase; *Musical Pig* (1966), a comical story of an operatic pig that finally finds a friend but at a steep price (he's eaten); and *The Bird and the Worm*, a *Pink Panther*-like series for children. Other animated characters for children included Grgic's whimsical canine, MaxiCat, and the popular Professor Balthazar series. In the late 1960s, Grgic moved to Canada and switched to advertising films and university teaching.

VIII: 1961–70: INTERNATIONAL EXPLOSION   EASTERN EUROPE: YUGOSLAVIA

Zagreb in the 1950s » 190

# ZAGREB IN THE 1960s: MOVING ON

The Zagreb studio gave its animators a remarkable degree of independence, which in the hands of many artists resulted in very personal films. Nedeljko Dragic was a well-known cartoonist and became one of Zagreb Film's most acclaimed artists. He made widely divergent films, but always with a very distinctive voice. His first film, *Elegy* (1965), was based on one of his comic strips. A prisoner stares sadly into a courtyard from behind the bars of his cell's small window. As the years go by, the growth of a single red flower gives him hope. In a later film, *Way to Your Neighbor* (1981), Dragic perfectly set up his punch line as a man dresses for just another day at the office, only to climb into a tank at the end of the film.

## Animation for Adults

Many of the animated films from Zagreb were decidedly not for children. *The Fly* (1967), for example, by the successful team of Aleksandar Marks and Vladimir Jutrisa, was a Kafka-like tale about a man and a fly butting heads, but ending up as equals. Some later films, like *Plop* (1987), directed by one of Zagreb's zaniest animators, Zlatko Pavlinic, use nudity as part of the element of surprise. In this one a man picks up a girl in a bar and takes her home, expecting her to do his housework: he's in for a big surprise. In *Dream Doll* (1979), a remarkable collaboration between Zlatko Grgic and the British animator Bob Godfrey, a man falls in love with a blow-up doll.

## International Hits

Other films, like *Satiemania* (1978) by Zdenko Gasparovic, and later *Album* (1983), by Kresimir Zimonic, are sophisticated renditions of the artist's personal musings. Based on the music of Eric Satie, *Satiemania* remains one of Zagreb's most internationally acclaimed films. It portrays the jungle of the big city – the supermarket, brothels and bars, and the ripple of water in simultaneous harmony and conflict – all moving to the mocking but lyrical music of Eric Satie. In *Album*, a young girl's childhood memories come to life as she thumbs through her family photograph album. Both *Satiemania* and *Dream Doll* were nominated for Oscars. Oscar-winning Dusan Vukotic also collaborated on other animators' films. For example, he wrote *Last Waltz in Old Mill* (1995), which was drawn and directed by Darko Krec.

While a limited-animation style was Zagreb Film's trademark, the fact that the films were artist-driven meant that animators were also free to break this convention. Films like *Satiemania*, *Album*, and *Diary* (1974) by Nedeljko Dragic, for example, are notable for their bold colors, full animation and lack of subtlety.

## End of an Era

The studio began to decline in the 1980s for a variety of reasons. First of all, there was a loss of talent. Vlado Kristl left for Germany in the 1960s. Vatroslav Mimica went back to

© Nedeljko Dragic, Elegy, Zagreb Film

**Elegy**

Nedeljko Dragic's touching short about a prisoner who regards the growth of a red flower beneath his window as a ray of hope won numerous prizes, including a Diploma in Venice, 1966.

## Speed Racer

*Speed Racer* was a 1966 creation of Tatsuo Yoshida, the founder of the Tatsunoko Productions studios in 1962. Yoshida had previously been a manga cartoonist, and one of his works was a licensed Japanese version of *Superman*. Yoshida used his American *Superman* art-style for his *Speed Racer* character designs.

## Gigantor

*Gigantor* was a 1963 adaptation of a popular 1950s and 1960s manga and was Japan's first giant-robot animation. Unlike most of his giant-robot successors, Gigantor did not have a human pilot who rode inside him; he was guided instead by a control-box in the hands of boy detective Jimmy Sparks.

## The Little Prince and the Eight-Headed Dragon

This was the sixth of Toei Doga's feature-length films. An action-adventure story, it drew on Japanese myth of a young god/prince named Susanoo, who embarks on an adventurous journey to the Underworld to find his dead mother Izanami. Along the way he fights off the Eight-Headed Dragon.

© Toei Doga

series; *Kitaro's* (*Scary Ghost Moon*) (1968), the first series on the theme of traditional Japanese supernatural-horror fantasy (although a comedy); *Sasuke* and *The Detective Stories of Sabu and Ichi* (1968), the first two significant series in the sixteenth–nineteenth century "samurai-ninja" historical-adventure genre; *Mrs Sazae* (1969), the first domestic comedy for housewives (still in production; it is the longest running animated TV series in the world); *Attack No. 1* (1969), the first sports-themed series (girls' school volleyball); and *Tomorrow's Joe* (1970), the first boys' sports series (boxing).

Many later prominent animators and animation directors began their careers during this decade, including Gisaburo Sugii (b. 1940), Rintaro (Shigeyuki Hayashi, b. 1941), Yoshiyuki Tomino (b. 1941) and Osamu Dezaki (b. 1943).

## Independent and Art Animation

In 1960 Tadahito Mochinaga created the M.O.M. Production Co. to produce puppet animation for America's Rankin/Bass. These ranged from TV series such as *The New Adventures of Pinocchio* (1960) and TV specials like *Rudolph the Red-Nosed Reindeer* (1964) to the theatrical feature *Mad Monster Party* (1967).

After Mochinaga's retirement in 1967, his staff (Takeo Nakamura, Koichi Oikawa and Tadanari Okamoto) kept together as Video Tokyo Productions, producing puppet and cut-paper animation. Many of their puppet-art films in the traditional Japanese *bunraku* style, such as Nakamura's *Torayan on the Boat* (1970), won international film-festival awards.

Japan's second animator to gain international acclaim through frequent worldwide festival screenings was Yoji Kuri (b. 1928). His cartoon shorts such as *The Human Zoo* (1962), *The Chair* (1962), *Samurai* (1965), *The Maniac Age* (1967) and *Flower* (1967) were short (often less than five minutes), sardonic line-art squiggles that influenced such animators as Canada's Richard Condie.

Two more notable animators were Sadao Tsukioka (b. 1939) and Tatsuo Shimamura (b. 1934). Tsukioka was the director of Toei's first TV animated series, *Ken the Wolf Boy* (1963–65); then he moved to Osamu Tezuka's Mushi Pro, where he worked on many TV series. Tezuka encouraged him to make his own art films, using Mushi's facilities, such as *Cigarettes and Ashes* and *The Story of Man*.

Shimamura also began as a Toei animator in 1958, but soon left to work independently. His films include *A Moonlit Night and Eyeglasses* (1966), *Fantasy City* (1967), *Love* (1970) and *A Fantasy of Flames* (1989).

It was during the late 1960s that the word "anime" (from the American and European words for animation) began to replace the Japanese word "doga" (moving drawings) in common usage.

Tadahito Mochinga » 142   Japanese Art Animation » 174

Osamu Tezuka (1928–89), honored with such titles as "the God of Comics" *(Manga no Kamisama)* and "the Disney of Japan", was born in Osaka to a medical family. It was assumed that he would become a doctor (and he did obtain his doctorate in medicine in 1961, although he never practiced), but while at Osaka University he began his first published comic strip in 1946. In 1947 his *New Treasure Island* became a best-selling manga and revolutionized the Japanese manga industry by its use of cinematic art direction, such as dramatic camera angles, pans and close-ups instead of static imagery. Tezuka acknowledged the influence of American animation by Disney and the Fleischers, as well as Wan Bros.' *Princess with the Iron Fan* and Seo's wartime *Momotaro* films.

## A Multitude of Influences

Beginning in the 1950s Tezuka became Japan's leading comic-book creator, in both popularity and influence. He was incredibly prolific, creating an estimated 150,000 pages of manga art during his lifetime. He created for all genres throughout the 1980s, including comics (and picture books) for infants; boys' adventure; girls' romantic fantasy; adult drama, including political thrillers; adult erotic humor and drama; cartoon adaptations of classic literature, such as Dostoyevsky's *Crime and Punishment*, and biography, such as the lives of Beethoven and the Buddha; and sci-fi as social satire. He actively promoted the concept that cartoon art is not a medium merely for children's entertainment. Tezuka became a celebrity by the mid-1950s, appearing in magazine articles and on TV as Japan's highest-earning artist of the decade.

In 1959 Toei Doga began a theatrical feature adaptation of Tezuka's *My Son Goku* (manga serialization, 1952–59), his take on the Chinese Monkey King legend. Tezuka was named a co-director, and although he later said his association with *Alakazam the Great* (1960) was more for publicity than actual production, it did inspire him to create his own animation studio. He felt that he could match the quality of the American new limited-animation TV cartoons, and he had his own 10-year backlog of popular manga to draw upon.

## Mushi Production Company

Tezuka's Mushi Production Co., Ltd. was created during 1962. Its first work was the arty *Stories on a Street Corner* (1962) for the Mainichi Film Festival. Its next was the New Year's Day 1963 premiere of the TV cartoon animated *Astro Boy* (syndicated in the US beginning September 1963). It was an immense success, running for four years with

### Pictures at an Exhibition

Tezuka's response to Disney's *Fantasia* used the 10 musical sequences of Mussorgsky's *Pictures at an Exhibition* as accompaniment to artistic satires of modern themes such as "War", "Politics", "Capitalism", and "Vapid Media Personalities".

### Astro Boy

Created by Dr Tenma (Dr Boynton) to replace his dead son, Astro Boy was sold to a robot circus when the inventor realized he could never grow up like a real boy. He was rescued from abuse by Ringmaster Hamegg (Cacciatore) by kindly Dr Ochanomizu (Elefun), who helped Astro Boy develop his human characteristics and use his powers against evil and for humankind, but also to stand up for "robot rights" against anti-robot prejudice. Tezuka was a pioneer in using his popular cartoons to advocate equal rights for all humanity. The original 1963–66 *Astro Boy* TV series was remade in 1980–81 and again in 2003–04.

*Princess With the Iron Fan* » 114  Japanese Art Animation » 174

# RALPH BAKSHI & FRITZ THE CAT

© Aurica Finance Company, Black Ink, Fritz Productions, Steve Krantz Productions

Brooklyn-born Ralph Bakshi (b. 1938) gained international notoriety for the first X-rated animated feature, *Fritz the Cat* (1972), which was based on Robert Crumb's underground comic-book character. It not only established the viability of adult animation, but also was a reminder that feature animation could also be an outlet for personal expression.

**Fritz the Cat**

Starting life as a character in comics, *Fritz the Cat* only made it to the big screen in 1972 in the first ever X-rated animation feature of the same name. It was only a modest commercial success.

## Beginnings

Bakshi began his career in animation at Terrytoons, where he directed such TV series as *Deputy Dawg* and became its creative director when he created *The Mighty Heroes* (1966) series. He then became head of Paramount Cartoon Studios during its final days, where he directed such shorts as *Marvin Digs* (1967) and *Mini Squirts* (1968). He was then hired by Steve Krantz Productions to take over direction and production of the *Rocket Robin Hood* and *Spider-Man* TV series.

Perhaps inspired by the success of George Dunning's *Yellow Submarine*, Krantz produced Bakshi's *Fritz the Cat*, his take on the 1960s counter-culture. Its huge financial success, combined with the controversy over its depiction of sex and drugs, woke people up to the possibilities of an animated film. Critics and moviegoers took it seriously. As Bakshi told Mike Barrier, "They treat it like film."

© Steve Krantz Productions

### The Nine Lives of Fritz the Cat

This follow-up to *Fritz the Cat* was released in 1974, but original director Ralph Bakshi was no longer involved. This was the last film to feature Fritz.

### Heavy Traffic

Mixing live action with animation, *Heavy Traffic* was released in 1973 to considerable acclaim. Originally X-rated, the film follows a Jewish-Italian man as he grows up in a tough area of New York.

### American Pop

Following several generations of a troubled but musically talented family, *American Pop* is an animated guide through music from the pre-jazz age through soul, 1950s rock, drug-laden psychedelia and punk, finally ending with the onset of new wave in the early 1980s.

© Columbia Pictures Corporation, Polyc International BV

## Mixed Fortunes

Bakshi next made *Heavy Traffic* (1973), which many consider his finest film. In it, he uses the tale of a struggling white cartoonist-animator to depict the underside of life in New York. Enjoying his new-found celebrity, he formed Bakshi Productions and spoke frequently of the expanding possibilities offered to the animation film-maker. However, his next film, *Hey Good Lookin'* (1975), was shelved after some disastrous previews, only to be unsuccessfully revised for release in 1982.

© Steve Krantz Productions, Orion Pictures

Accusations of racism regarding *Coonskin* (a.k.a. *Street Fight*) (1975), which had its premiere at New York's Museum of Modern Art, caused Paramount Pictures to drop the film, and subsequent distribution was limited.

Bakshi tackled fantasy with *Wizards* (1977), a post-apocalyptic sci-fi fantasy that failed at the box office, he had one of his biggest financial successes with *Lord of the Rings* (1978), which capitalized on the popularity of author J. R. R. Tolkien. However, it was criticized for its extensive use of Rotoscoping, which seemed to rob the visuals of the vitality of his earlier films.

*American Pop* (1981) was an unsuccessful attempt to provide a picture of American popular music in the twentieth century through the story of a Russian-Jewish family. And the failure of *Fire and Ice* (1983), created with famed fantasy illustrator Frank Frazetta, made Bakshi turn his attention to TV.

## Return to Form

It was with the live-action/animated Rolling Stones' 'Harlem Shuffle' music video in 1986 that Bakshi seemed to find himself again. He went on to produce *Mighty Mouse: The New Adventures* (1987–88), the groundbreaking TV series that jump-started the career of John Kricfalusi and laid the groundwork for a renaissance in television animation.

He briefly returned to movies with the poorly received live-action/animated *Cool World* (1992), before returning to TV with the live-action movie *The Cool and the Crazy* (1994). After the short-lived animated sci-fi detective series *Spicy City* (1997), Bakshi left animation and devoted himself to painting.

# SATURDAY MORNING BLUES

TV animation in the US was essentially relegated to a Saturday-morning ghetto during the 1970s. Adding to the medium's misery was the development of overseas production – American studios were farming production work mainly to Japan or Australia – and the triumph of various parent groups in their efforts to strip all of the fun from cartoons, essentially removing all slapstick action and comic violence, and injecting educational and pro-social messages into the narratives. Animation was now widely perceived as a children's medium. The poor reputation of Saturday-morning cartoons comes from the programming created during this decade: cheap productions, poor animation and weak writing were aimed at an undiscriminating audience. And on top of all that: Action for Children's Television (ACT).

## Imposing Restrictions

ACT grew out of the suburban Boston living room of housewife and mother Peggy Charren, who used her organization to lobby Washington to impose new rules on kids' programming – cartoons in particular. Their voice grew louder as the decade wore on, and their campaign for change was very effective. Soon, network executives began dictating the content of the programming they chose to air. Independent thinking and artistic genius were no longer welcome – Jay Ward, Bob Clampett and other top talents left the field to the remaining cartoon factories: Hanna-Barbera, Filmation, DePatie-Freleng and Rankin-Bass.

Hanna-Barbera's *Scooby-Doo, Where Are You?* premiered in 1969, and became a staple of Saturday-morning TV for the subsequent decade. The program, about a quartet of teenage mystery solvers and their mascot – a fearful, lumbering Great Dane named Scooby-Doo – had the right combination of suspense, laughs and character types to appeal to children at the time.

*Scooby-Doo*'s success led to a succession of similar ideas and derivative series: *Amazing Chan & the Chan Clan* (1972), *Goober and the Ghost Chasers* (1973), *Butch Cassidy and the Sundance Kids* (1973) and *Clue Club* (1976), to name but a few.

## Competition

Hanna-Barbera's chief rival at this time was Filmation, which had scored a hit with their rock'n'roll revision of *The Archies* (1968–78). Typical American teenagers Archie Andrews, Veronica Lodge, Betty Cooper and Jughead Jones had been comic book stars for over 20 years when the Filmation series propelled them into even greater fame – a cartoon show that spawned one of the biggest-selling records of 1969, 'Sugar Sugar'.

Hanna-Barbera fought back by adapting another group of Archie Comics stars, *Josie and the Pussy Cats* (1970), which combined rock'n'roll music with *Scooby-*

**The Archies**

Originally appearing in comic-book form in 1941, *The Archies* featured red-headed Archie Andrews as a "typical" American teenager along with his friends at Riverdale High.

**Jughead and Big Ethel**

Archie made the transition to the small screen in 1968 in a cartoon series that ran in various incarnations for about 10 years. Popular supporting characters included Jughead Jones and his nemesis, Big Ethel.

© Filmation Associates

*Doo*-like mystery – creating the ultimate hybrid cartoon show of the 1970s. For the rest of the decade, the studios took their cues from those elements: a pre-sold character or celebrity teamed with rock music and mystery. The results: *Partridge Family 2200 AD* (1974), *The Brady Kids* (1972), *The Jackson Five* (1971), *The Osmonds* (1972), *Sabrina and the Groovie Goolies* (1970), *The New Adventures of Gilligan* (1974) and *Will the Real Jerry Lewis Please Sit Down?* (1970). Saturday-morning cartoons were at their emptiest, most soulless extreme.

There were some exceptions. *Fat Albert and the Cosby Kids* (Filmation, 1972) was a cartoon with an educational message – but it was inspired by a talented creator, comedian Bill Cosby. With characters you could relate to and strong entertainment values, this series delighted ACT members because it proved that pro-social animation could compete commercially.

## Superheroes Return

Superheroes had not lost their appeal, however. Hanna-Barbera picked up DC's costumed characters and refashioned the Justice League as the educator-approved, family-friendly Super Friends. Now, instead of fighting criminal jokers and madmen intent on destroying the world, Superman, Batman, Robin, Aquaman and Wonder Woman would solve mysteries created by well-meaning scientists whose experiments have run amok.

Other 1970s superheroics were performed by the funny animals in *Hong Kong Fooey* (1974), real-life celebrities in *The Harlem Globetrotters* (1970) and *I Am The Greatest: The Adventures of Muhammad Ali* (1977), or other comic-book rivals like *The New Fantastic Four* (1978).

American TV animation lost its promise and sank to new depths during this dark decade. And it would get a lot worse before a new wave in the late 1980s would return its potential. But 1970s series like *Fat Albert* and *Scooby-Doo* – even the Super Friends – have endured the test of time to become kitsch classics to a generation who were raised on them.

### The Groovie Goolies

A cartoon series about a group of ghouls and their various adventures at Horrible Hall, *The Groovie Goolies* combined with *Sabrina the Teenage Witch* for a brief series in 1970. Following the demise of *Sabrina and the Goolies*, the two strands became individual programs. The characters of Count Drac, Missy and Wolfie are shown here.

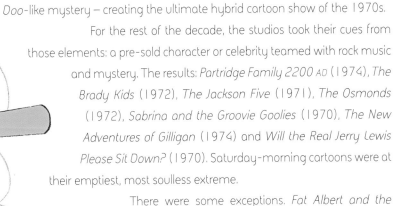

# THE GREAT WHITE NORTH

By the early 1960s, the NFB had become known as much for its cartoons as for its experimental films. These cartoons, equal to those of Hollywood's Golden Age, include *The Great Toy Robbery* (1964); Gerald Potterton's *My Financial Career* (1962) and *Christmas Cracker* (1963); Kaj Pindal's comic masterpieces *I Know an Old Lady who Swallowed a Fly* (1964) and *What On Earth!* (1966); *Evolution* (1971); *Propaganda Message* (1974); and Zlatko Grgic's *Hot Stuff* (1971).

### An International Flavour

In 1966, the NFB set up a separate French animation studio. Favoring individual expression, by the 1970s the studio had become home to Jacques Drouin, master of pinscreen animation (*Mindscape*, 1976); puppet animator Co Hoedeman (Oscar winner for *Sand Castle*, 1977); Pierre Hebert (*Memories of War*, 1982); Paul Driessen (*An Old Box*, 1975); and Peter Foldes (*The Hunger*, 1974, an early computer animated film).

Born in Seattle, Washington, in 1946, Caroline Leaf joined the French animation studio to direct *The Owl Who Married a Goose* (1974), and also directed *The Street* (1976) for the English studio. Based on Mordecai Richler's short story, Leaf used the technique of animating colored oil on glass directly under the camera. Animating colored sand, Leaf adapted Franz Kafka's *The Metamorphosis of Mr Samsa* in 1977.

Ishu Patel arrived at the NFB in 1970 from India. Working with various techniques directly under the camera, Patel was nominated for two Academy Awards for *Bead Game* (1977) and *Paradise* (1984).

*Special Delivery* (1978) won directors John Weldon and Eunice Macaulay an Academy Award. The following year the NFB again won an Oscar for *Every Child* (1979), directed by Eugene Fedorenko. The most beloved animated film in Canada is *The Sweater* (1976), directed by Sheldon Cohen and based on Roch Carrier's short story of a young Montreal Canadiens fan forced to wear a Toronto Maple Leafs jersey.

### Frederic Back

The NFB was not the only government agency producing animation. Société Radio-Canada had formed an animation department in 1968.

Born in Saarbrucken, Germany, in 1924, Frederic Back joined Société Radio-Canada as a graphic artist in 1952. In 1970 Back directed his first film (with Graeme Ross), *Abracadabra*. He followed this up with *Inon*, or the *Conquest of Fire* (1972), *The Creation of the Birds* (1973), *Illusion* (1974) and *Taratata* (1976).

With *All-Nothing* (1978) Back began using the technique of animating with colored pencils directly on frosted cels – essentially creating moving paintings. *All-Nothing* received an Oscar nomination, the first of four for Back.

© 1974 National Film Board of Canada

**The Owl Who Married a Goose**

In this film Caroline Leaf interprets an Inuit legend about an owl who falls in love with a goose and meets a tragic end. The film is animated using sand and the soundtrack features Inuit Indian voices imitating bird sounds.

© 1979 National Film Board of Canada

## Every Child

This six-minute animation was made for the United Nations to celebrate UNICEF's Declaration of Children's Rights and the International Year of the Child. One of the ten principles of the Declaration is illustrated in the film, namely that every child is entitled to a name and a nationality.

A hymn to the traditions and culture of Quebec, *Crac!* (1981) tells the story of a rocking chair that has been passed through a family, but when discarded finds itself again the center of attention at an art museum. Influenced by the painters Degas and Monet, and by Quebec folklore, *Crac!* won Back his first Academy Award.

*The Man Who Planted Trees* (1987) is Back's masterpiece. The story by Jean Giono is of Elzear Bouffier, a shepherd from the Maritime Alps who tirelessly plants thousands of oak trees and transforms a barren plain into a paradise. If *Crac!* is a hymn, then *The Man Who Planted Trees* is a poem. It won Back his second Oscar. *The Mighty River* (1993) continued Back's environmental concerns, visually documenting the development of the St Lawrence Seaway.

## Successful Decade

Commercial animation in Canada bloomed in the 1970s. Contract work for American broadcasters had been performed in Canada since the early 1960s. After leaving the NFB, Gerald Potterton set up his own studio in the late 1960s to create both live-action and animation projects. After producing a number of TV specials, Potterton directed the feature film *Heavy Metal* (1980). With a very short production schedule, sequences were subcontracted to studios across Canada and around the world.

In the early 1970s Michael Hirsch, Patrick Loubert and Clive Smith formed Nelvana. Their first successes, *Cosmic Christmas* (1977) and *The Devil and Daniel Mouse* (1978), led to the feature film *Rock and Rule* (1983). Involving one of the greatest staffs in animation, mostly homegrown talent, *Rock and Rule* (a.k.a. *Ring of Power*) featured some outstanding animation and design. Unfortunately, the film went way over budget and took so long to finish that by the time it was released much of the film's music was passé. It brought Nelvana to the brink of bankruptcy. The studio turned to series work to survive, and would go on to be a major force in TV animation during the 1980s.

TV Co-Production » 378

# INDEPENDENTS GROW

During the 1970s and 1980s, Will Vinton (b. 1948) almost single-handedly revitalized stop-motion animation with his trademarked claymation shorts and helped establish the viability of regional animation in the US. While studying architecture and film, he came under the influence of the visionary Spanish architecture of Antonio Gaudi's organic forms. After working in live-action, he experimented with clay animation, which eventually resulted in his collaborating with Bob Gardiner on the Oscar-winning short *Closed Mondays* (1974).

### Will Vinton Productions

He then set up Will Vinton Productions in Portland, Oregon, where over the next decade he made a series of shorts that made his reputation and earned him Oscar nominations for *Martin the Cobbler* (1976), *Rip Van Winkle* (1978) and *The Great Cognito* (1982). The latter, which became his signature film, is a *tour de force* in which the title character undergoes a series of rapid metamorphoses as he delivers a comic monologue.

Among his other short films were *Mountain Music* (1975), a version of Antoine de Saint Exupéry's *The Little Prince* (1979) and *Dinosaur* (1980). The failure of his sole feature effort, *The Adventures of Mark Twain* (1984), essentially a collection of short films, was eclipsed by the acclaim for his John Fogerty 'Vanz Kant Danz' (1985) music video and the 'Speed Demon' sequence in Michael Jackson's *Moonwalker* feature (1988).

### Commercial Success

Toward the end of this period, Vinton began leaving directing chores to others and eventually concentrated on the creative aspects of running the studio. As he did this, the company achieved great popularity for its California Raisins commercials, which led to two prime-time TV specials: *Meet the Raisins* (1988) and *The Raisins Sold Out!* (1990). In 1987, he won Emmys for *A Claymation Christmas Celebration* and for the animated/live-action sequence in the popular *Moonlighting* TV show.

Will Vinton Studios eventually expanded into digital animation, especially for TV commercials, and had moderate success with *The PJs*, a prime-time TV series co-produced with Eddie Murphy using traditional puppet animation. However, the failure of a subsequent prime-time series, *Gary and Mike*, and the collapse of the market for TV commercials led to Vinton losing control of the studio in 2003.

### Bob Godfrey

Bob Godfrey (b. 1921) has been one of Britain's most distinctive comic talents, emerging from the same irreverent spirit that energized the free cinema movement of the 1960s.

© Will Vinton Studios

**California Raisins**

The California Raisins were created from different colors of Van Aken clay, including yellow, blue and white, resulting in Raisin Purple. The Raisins had a trademark song 'I Heard It Through The Grapevine', (a Marvin Gaye classic), and were animated with the help of reference footage of actors dancing.

© Bob Godfrey

**Bob Godfrey**

Specializing in hand-drawn media, Bob Godfrey is famous for his distinctive "wobbling" cartoons, which are created using a technique called boiling. His witty, fast-paced animations have included several popular series for children, including *Henry's Cat* and *Roobarb and Custard*.

**Great**

As well as highly successful children's cartoons, Godfrey also did a number of more adult-themed animations. *Great* (1975) is a breakneck sprint through Isambard Kingdom Brunel's life and achievements. Using hand-drawn, mixed-media animation, it won an Academy Award in 1975 and a BAFTA in 1976.

**Roobarb and Custard**

The first animated television series ever to be made in the UK was *Roobarb and Custard*, a series of cartoons featuring a cat and dog that has achieved cult status since its first airing in 1974. The characters in the Roobarb cartoons were colored in with nothing more sophisticated than Magic Markers.

He has proved himself equally adept at adult-oriented shorts – lampooning British attitudes, especially sexual attitudes – and children's TV series.

Born in Australia, Godfrey came to the UK as a baby. He began his animation career in 1949 as a background artist for the W.M. Larkin Studio on promotional and technical films, and directed his first film, *The Big Parade*, in 1952 with Keith Learner. In 1954, he joined up with Jeff Hale to form Biographic Films, which made some of the first commercials for Britain's ITV, as well as many cinema advertisements. This allowed him the freedom to do a series of personal films that he became identified with, including *Polygamous Polonius* (1959) and *Do-It-Yourself Cartoon Kit* (1961). These films showed the influence of *The Goons*, along with his interest in political satire and British morals, sexual and otherwise. While visually rather crude, their quintessential British humor put them very much outside the dominant American mode so prevalent at the time; as such, they helped establish a uniquely British school of animation.

## Variety of Subjects

In 1964, he formed Bob Godfrey Films to gain more control over his work, which included such mock-erotic films as *Henry 'Til 5* (1970), *Kama Sutra Rides Again* (1971) and *Dream Doll* (1979), made with Zagreb Studio's Zlatko Grgic. His most ambitious film was *Great* (1975), the Oscar-winning half-hour satirical biography of British engineer Isambard Kingdom Brunel.

In addition to his theatrical efforts, Godfrey was also active in TV. He directed four episodes of *The Beatles'* TV series in 1966, and in 1974 wrote and narrated the highly influential *The Do-It-Yourself Film Animation Kit* TV series, which Aardman's Nick Park said was instrumental in getting him into animation. More recently, he made *Millennium – the Musical* (1999), a satirical TV special profiling Margaret Thatcher. He has also produced several popular children's series, including *Roobarb and Custard* (1974), which was based on the stories of Grange Calveley and has become a cult classic; *Henry's Cat* (1983); and *Kevin Saves the World* (2002).

# RENÉ LALOUX

French artist René Laloux (1929–2004) had already determined he would dedicate his life to painting when he was invited to create an experimental workshop at Cheverny Court, a private psychiatric clinic. Here, with the assistance of the inmates, he produced a jarring 14-minute film, *Les Dents du Singe* ('The Monkey's Teeth', 1960), involving a primate having his teeth forcibly extracted.

## Clinical Experiment

By adapting a number of the patients' drawings, Laloux and his students managed to construct a 16 mm (0.6 in) animated cut-out film as a clinical experiment. The end product was seen and bought by Fréderic Rossif and, spurred on by his success at making animated films, Laloux took the money for *The Monkey's Teeth* and sank it into a second project.

His next film, *Temps Morts* ('Dead Times', 1964), conveyed another somber message and was described as "a visual perception of death and its consequences". In collaboration with post-surrealist painter and writer Roland Topor (b. 1938), he next presented a bizarre gothic-horror tale concerning a town overrun with colossal snails entitled *Les Escargots* ('The Snails', 1965).

## Adventures in Science Fiction

By the early 1970s, he was embarking on his most challenging project to date, lending his distinctive style of art to an adaptation of Stefan Wul's popular 1957 science-fiction parable *Ome en Serie*. Retitled *La Planète Sauvage* (a.k.a *Fantastic Planet*, *The Savage Planet* or *Planet of Incredible Creatures*, 1973), the story deals with existence on the planet Ygam. The Oms, a race of humanoid creatures (the name "Ome" is derived from "homme", the French word for man), struggle to rid themselves of domination from the 39-ft- (12-m-) high, blue-skinned "Draags" who treat them as domestic pets.

The Draags are higher beings who dedicate their leisure time to meditation and keeping the population of the Oms down by culling them every so often.

### La Planète Sauvage

Released in 1973, *La Planète Sauvage* is a surreal tale that takes place on a faraway planet where giants rule and tiny humans must fight for equality and their lives. It depicts the eternal human struggle for freedom, showing what happens when the human capacity to think and learn is suppressed.

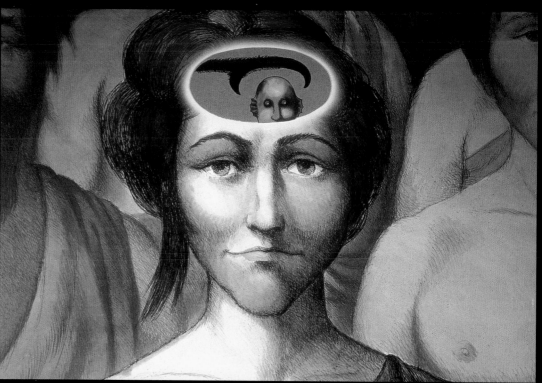

© Krátky Film Praha, Les Films Armorial, Service de la Recherche ORTF, Ceskoslovensky Filmexport

### Hugo the Hippo

Hugo is put on trial for causing damage to a village, but the Sultan denounces his persecutor, Aban Khan, and reminds the court of the hippos' invaluable past service. A dark and often bizarre film, Hugo the Hippo has nonetheless become a cult classic of sorts.

### Fight

Winner of the Palme d'Or for best short film at the 1977 Cannes Film Festival, Fight was one of several very successful animations to come from Hungarian animator Marcell Jankovics.

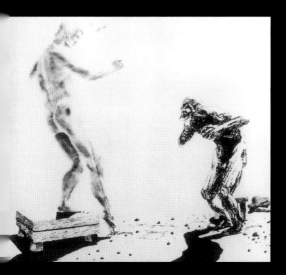

Tamás Szabó Sípos's *Let Me Explain* took on a more educational function. In each episode, a character named Dr Brain set out to explain the world. In one episode, for example, Dr Brain, in a jovial and ironic manner, explains the basics of economics.

The 1970s also saw other TV productions, including *Tails the Cat-Chaser*, which used a cut-out technique; *Kukori and Kotkoda*; *Mirr-Murr the Tom-Cat*; *Elek Mekk — Jack-of-All-Trades*; and *Tales from Crow Hill*. In 1978, Marcell Jankovics launched a new adult series called *Hungarian Folk Tales*.

## Not Short on Shorts

Despite the increasingly commercial nature of the studio, Pannonia continued to encourage and support the production of short animation films. While the older generation concerned themselves primarily with ethical and philosophical questions, the younger generation turned their attentions to modern challenges and realities. Among the highlights of this period are *Moon Flight* (1975) and *Panic* (1978), both by Sándor Reisenbüchler; *Wave Length* (1971) by György Kovásznai; *Modern Sports Coaching* (1970) by Bela Ternovsky; and two films that won prestigious Golden Palm awards at the Cannes Film Festival, Sándor Reisenbüchler's *1812* (1973) and Marcell Jankovic's *Fight* (1977).

A new generation of animators emerged during the 1970s, notably Kati Macskássy, daughter of Hungarian animation pioneer Gyula Macskássy, who made quality children's films including the acclaimed *Push Button* (1973) and *I Think Life's Great Fun* (1976). Péter Szoboszlay made the humorous *Hey, You* (1976), Csaba Szórády produced *Rondino* (1977) and Csaba Varga took a group of amateur film-makers from Pécs and formed the animation studio IXILON in 1974. Varga was commissioned by Pannonia to produce films and to establish a studio in Pécs. The studio became known for its bold graphic style and adult-tailored films. In 1988, the studio would become the famous Varga Studio.

## Marcell Jankovics

One of the most successful and interesting Hungarian animators of this period was Marcell Jankovics. Born in Budapest, he made his first film, *The Legend of Saint Silvester* in 1964. Since then, Jankovics has alternated with great ease between children's films, television series, feature films and his own personal short films. His short films have garnered wide international acclaim and have themselves been diverse in tone, ranging from satire in *Deep Water* (1971) to heavier, existentialist films like *SOS* (1970), *Sisyphus* (1973) and *The Fight* (1977).

TV animation was dominant during the 1970s, with most theatrical features being big-screen spin-offs. Some did not even present new stories, but merely summarized the TV story line. The most notable exceptions to this standard were the two *Lupin III* features produced by TMS Entertainment Ltd (a.k.a. Tokyo Movie Shinsha): *Lupin III: The Secret of Mamo* (1978), directed by Soji Yoshikawa, and *The Castle of Cagliostro* (1979), written and directed by Hayao Miyazaki. The most significant advance in TV animation was the upgrading of its target audience from children to adolescents and young adults. The distinctive art styles of manga cartoonists Go Nagai (b. 1945), Leiji Matsumoto (b. 1938) and "Monkey Punch" (Kazuhiko Kato, 1937) became familiar fixtures on the small screen.

## Space-Age Animation

Nagai created the concept of heroic teenagers who donned mechanical battle armor or piloted transformable vehicles and fought as giant robots to protect the world (Japan) from ruthless conquering outer-space armies. The first was *Mazinger Z*, produced by Toei Doga in 222 episodes under three titles from 1972 until 1977. By the end of the decade, there were 40 giant-robot cartoon series created by practically every TV animation studio.

A major variant was introduced by Nippon Sunrise studio writer/director Yoshiyuki Tomino in 1979 with *Mobile Suit Gundam*, which recast the giant robots from unique superhero suits to more realistic futuristic military combat vehicles, and the adversaries from humans versus demonic aliens to warring human space nations.

Nagai also pioneered TV animation with supernatural horror, with *Devilman* (1972), and the first risqué-humor adventure series, *Cutey Honey* (1973), featuring a buxom teen girl (actually an android) whose clothing briefly disappeared when she changed from one costumed disguise to another.

## Small-Screen Adventures

Leiji Matsumoto specialised in interstellar sci-fi adventure series, notably the long-running *Space Battleship Yamato* (1974), plus several sequels, *Space Pirate Captain Harlock* (1978) and *Galaxy Express 999* (1978). Monkey Punch was known primarily for his long-running manga *Lupin III* about a charismatic international jewel thief. Designed for adults rather than for children, its TV animated series ran for over 200 episodes throughout the 1970s and mid-1980s, evolving into a series of annual animated features that continue today.

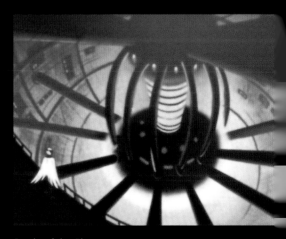

Other major TV animation included Tatsuo Yoshida's sci-fi superhero team in *Battle of the Planets* (1972); the adolescent tear-jerker romance *Candy Candy* (1976–79); *The Rose of Versailles* (a.k.a. *Lady Oscar*, 1979), based upon Ryoko Ikeda's historical romance set at the court of Louis XVI; and a TV cartoon series of Fujio Fujiko's manga for children about the time-travelling robot toy cat *Doraemon* (1979)

**Battle of the Planets**

This began as the Japanese 1972 TV cartoon series *Science Ninja Team Gatchaman* (first and third images). It was transformed for American TV in 1978 by a team led by Disney/Hanna-Barbera veteran Jameson Brewer and *Flintstones* director Alan Dinehart (second image: robot 7-Zark-7, an American addition to the cast).

© Renzo Kinoshita/Studio Lotus

## Made in Japan

*Made In Japan* won the Grand Prix at the New York International Animation Festival in 1972. Renzo Kinoshita began working as an independent animator in 1967 making films with powerful messages to contemporary society. Kinoshita's wife Sayoko worked with him on his films often helping with in-betweening, coloring and making puppets.

## Independent Shorts and Puppet Animation

In art animation, Renzo Kinoshita (1936–97) began as a TV animator in the 1960s, but under the influence of Tezuka and Kuri he switched to making independent short films for festival screenings. His masterpiece is the anti-nuclear warfare *Pika-Don* (1978); others include *What on Earth is He?* (1971), *Made In Japan* (1972), *Invitation to Death* (1973), *The Calculating Machine* (1973) and *The Japanese* (1977). He was a co-founder in 1985 of the bi-annual Hiroshima International Animation Festival, which he directed with his wife Sayoko until his death.

Kihachiro Kawamoto, "the Magician of Puppet Animation", began at Tadahito Mochinaga's puppet studio in the 1950s. In 1962 he went to Czechoslovakia to study under puppet animator Jiri Trnka. His first film, *Breaking Branches is Forbidden* (1968), was the first of his many films to win international-festival prizes. In 1972, Kawamoto and fellow Mochinaga veteran Tadanari Okamoto began an annual show touring major Japanese cities, featuring both puppet and cut-paper animated films and live-puppet plays of Japanese folk tales and classic drama. Kawamoto's films included *The Devil* (1972), *The Journey* (1973), *The Life of a Poet* (1974), *Dojoji Temple* (1976) and *House of Flames* (1979). In the 1980s and 1990s the governmental NHK station funded his puppet dramatizations of classic Japanese and Chinese literature.

© Kihachiro Kawamoto

## Dojoji Temple

*Dojoji Temple* is a traditionally inspired Japanese story about a woman's passion. The woman's emotional state is cleverly communicated by changes in the lighting of her face. The style of the watercolour backdrops resembles the narrative picture scrolls of traditional Japanese art.

Tadanari Okamoto's first puppet film, *Strange Medicine*, won the 1965 Ofuji Award. He was not as prolific as Kawamoto, but his puppet and cut-paper works include such international festival favorites as *Home My Home* (1970), *The Flowers and the Mole* (1971), *The Mochi-Mochi Tree* (1971), *The Crab's Vengeance on the Monkey* (1972), *Praise Be to Small Ills* (1973), *Water Seed* (1975), *The Bridge of Strength* (1976), *The Magic Fox* (1982) and *A Well-Ordered Restaurant* (1991), which was completed posthumously by his assistants.

# FINDING AN IDENTITY

Two Australian animators are having lunch. The eager, younger one states, "Animation is imagination!" His companion — older, more pragmatic — replies, "Yes, but is it local imagination or imported imagination?"

© Air Programus International Studio

## The Influence of TV

Australian animation took a long time to become a viable, substantial industry. Before the modern telecommunications age, Australian animation suffered from entrenched national problems: a tiny population (and consequently a too-limited market), a lack of the centrally concentrated resources of Hollywood and the ever-present "tyranny of distance". Despite attempts by pioneers like Eric Porter (1910–83) and Melbourne's Owen Brothers (Will and Harrie) to make indigenous theatrical cartoons, little of major animation consequence happened until the advent of television in 1956.

Suddenly, TV commercials and a constant supply of flashy promos and animated network logos were required, and the business began to benefit from regular work. Very quickly, that work matched international standards, employing a wide variety of graphic styles, ranging from traditional character animation to more UPA-inspired modeling, to outright experimental design work.

Meanwhile, in America the TV cartoon business mushroomed following the huge success of Hanna-Barbera's *Ruff and Reddy* and *Huckleberry Hound* shows. By the end of the 1950s the demand for episodic cartoon product was rapidly outstripping the supply of American animation talent.

## Slice of the American Pie

To solve this dilemma, producers like Al Brodax in New York and Jay Ward on the West Coast began subcontracting animation of their shows to outfits in Mexico, Canada and Holland. Storyboards and soundtracks were prepared in the States, but the labor-intensive drawing process was executed overseas under American supervision. Wanting a piece of this lucrative pie, Australia established its credentials as another cost-effective outsourcing center. Artist Gus McLaren recalled, "It wasn't just a matter of us being cheaper; there was a dearth of animators in America."

In the early 1960s the first examples of Down Under "runaway production" occurred when the animation wing of Artransa Park Studios (busy with

**King Arthur and the Square Knights of the Round Table**

In 1966, 39 half-hour episodes were made of this all-Australian production. This was API's most successful series and was syndicated in the US by Twentieth Century Fox and sold to 14 countries. Zoran Janjic, an animator originally from the Zagreb Studios, directed the series.

*Tron*, released by Disney in 1982, was the movie that introduced computer animation to the masses. Directed by Steven Lisberger, the film was a visual delight, and featured ground-breaking computer-generated imagery (CGI) combined with live-action.

## The Story

*Tron* is about a brash young computer hacker named Flynn (Jeff Bridges) who owns a video arcade. Flynn was a star programmer at Encom, a stereotypical faceless corporation. A co-worker of Flynn's, named Dillenger (David Warner), stole Flynn's work and used it to get promoted. In the process, Dillenger also managed to get Flynn fired. Flynn enlists Alan and Lora (Bruce Boxleitner and Cindy Morgan), two friends and ex-colleagues, to help him break into Encom so he can prove Dillenger stole his work. While attempting to de-activate his stolen program, Flynn is beamed into the computer itself. There, he enters a computer-generated world where he must battle other programs in video-game-like combat in order to defeat the Master Control Program.

## Computer-Generated Magic

Unlike modern CGI films, which promise total realism, *Tron* saturated the audience in bright colors and unabashedly computer-generated visuals. The production design by Syd Mead, Dean Edward Mitzner and Jean "Moebius" Giraud gave a beautiful look of the inside of a computer that pre-dated such movies as *The Matrix* (1999) by decades. Some of the production design was dictated by the primitive state of computer animation at the time, which could only handle simple shapes and textures. The resulting film showed how good design could overcome any technical limitations.

The most successful parts of the film were those that took place within the computer itself. One of the most memorable scenes is the light-cycle sequence, where Flynn must pilot a CG motorcycle at breakneck speeds. The animation was truly stunning, and for the first time immersed theater audiences in the world of the video game.

© The Walt Disney Company

**Tron – storyboard**

In order for the production team to determine what would be required by way of computer-generated backgrounds, storyboards were drawn up to provide a blueprint for the action.

success story comes with Aardman Animations. Following screenings of their initial work on the BBC, Channel 4 offered to finance a series entitled *Conversation Pieces*. This series consisted of using a selection of 'vox pop' interviews, putting recorded words into the mouths of their animated characters. So successful were these *Conversation Pieces* that it led to another series entitled *Lip Synch*, featuring the *Creature Comforts* animals. This, in turn, led to the same characters being used for a series of hugely popular commercials, along with many other diversions that have been the backbone of Aardman.

Sadly, Channel 4's opportunity to create worthwhile television cartoons evaporated somewhere in the 1990s, and the system no longer exists to commission animated works of art. However, it was good while it lasted.

**Raymond Briggs' The Snowman illustration**

The film's success was helped by its original orchestral score by Howard Blake, Briggs's book avoided speech, and the film was reliant upon its images and music to move the story on, with occasional sound effects, such as the bells on a Christmas tree, or a motorbike.

# THE QUAY BROTHERS

Heavily influenced by Eastern European cinema (particularly the surrealist Czech puppet animator Jan Svankmajer), twin brothers Stephen and Timothy Quay (b. 1947) have rekindled the kind of Gothic photoplay typical of the 1930s with their surrealistic stop-motion puppet films.

### London-Bound

Natives of Norristown, Pennsylvania, the twins studied illustration at the Philadelphia College of Art, and in 1969 neatly avoided the draft by taking a course at London's Royal College of Art (RCA). They soon found London to be a cornucopia of decadence, overflowing with libraries, cinema, theater, opera, ballet and all the things that were not available in Norristown. When the course ended, and with money receding, the twins returned home and started preparing for a future visit.

During 1978, their friend and collaborator Keith Griffiths from the RCA informed the twins that he had managed to get them a grant from the British Film Institute so they would be able to make their first film. The Quays were soon back tramping the streets of London where, in 1980 with producer Keith Griffiths, they established their own studio. Their intention was to produce innovative puppet films that paid homage to the style of the early European puppeteers they so admired.

### Nocturna Artificiala

Their first venture, *Nocturna Artificiala* ('Artificial Nocturne', 1979), involves the slight story of a man who, staring from a window, is mesmerized by a trolley car passing through an ill-lit city at night. He is seen back in his room and awakens with a start when he falls from his chair. This film was inspired by the boys' stay in an Amsterdam hotel, where passing trams cast menacing shadows throughout the room.

*Nocturna Artificiala* accentuates several causes and effects that were to become apparent in the Quay brothers' subsequent films: sets dominated by darkness; bizarre, unexplained nightmarish happenings; and odd camera angles – in short, all the things that put one in mind of the early French, German or Polish animators of the 1930s. Even the subtitles appear in four separate languages.

The Quays have always claimed that they "want to make a world that is seen through a dirty pane of glass". This perhaps explains their macabre, half-lit, miniaturized domain and the eerie feeling their work creates.

**The Quay Brothers**

The brothers Quay tend to avoid words in their films, relying instead on sound, music, objects, movement and light to convey meaning. Renowned for their craftsmanlike methods and unusual sources of inspiration, they make puppets that look like old dolls abused by many generations of children, construct the sets, arrange the lighting and do the photography.

**Street of Crocodiles – character**

This film has a dreamlike quality to it, partly due to its highly stylized direction. It has a shallow plane of focus that intentionally keeps certain objects blurred and a camera that moves with conspicuous mechanical precision.

© Brothers Quay/BFI Production Board, Channel 4, Konnick Studios

**The Street of Crocodiles**

The world invented by the Quay brothers for *Crocodiles* was the color of an old photograph: sepia, dirty, dark yellow, and brown. It seemed as if it was a locked room or glass cabinet that nobody had opened for years – dusty and cobwebby, almost a mystical land.

## Street of Crocodiles

Their second film, *Ein Brudermord* ('A Fratricide', 1981), was founded on the writings of Franz Kafka. A series of animated documentaries built around people they held in high regard followed, capped by an affectionate homage to their particular hero in the documentary *The Cabinet of Jan Svankmajer – Prague's Alchemist of Film* (1984).

The claustrophobic *Street of Crocodiles* is perhaps their best-known work. Financed by the British Film Institute in conjunction with Channel 4 and based on a story by Polish writer Bruno Schulz, it depicts an aged museum watchman who, while on his rounds, falters at a kinescope machine. A drop of his saliva falls on the apparatus, putting it into motion, an action that also enlivens a puppet that severs his strings and begins to investigate the street of crocodiles. There he encounters a collection of foreboding doors leading to equally foreboding rooms, one of which contains a robotic sweatshop where the puppet is taken apart, redesigned and reclothed.

## Commercial Work

On the lighter side, the brothers have also been instrumental in providing pop promos for groups such as His Name Is Alive, Michael Penn, Sparklehorse, 16 Horsepower and Peter Gabriel's 'Sledgehammer' video. They also created a selection of innovative commercials for products such as Coca-Cola, MTV, Nikon, Slurpee and the Partnership for a Drug Free America.

The twins' more recent occupation has broadened to designing theater and opera sets, and in 1998 their staging for the Broadway production of Ionesco's *The Chairs* was nominated for a much-coveted Tony Award. In 1994 the Quays entered the world of live-action feature film-making with *Institute Benjamenta*, returning to animation in 2000 with the award-winning *In Absentia*, plus two dance films in 2002, *Duet* and *The Sandman*. Yet another departure from the animation tracks was the brothers' collaboration with composer Steve Martland in creating sets for a live event at the Tate Modern art museum in London.

# A CAULDRON OF TALENT

The 1980s were a bubbling cauldron of gifted young animated film-makers, partially due to colleges now including animation in their curriculum and partially due to the arrival of Channel 4 and their policy of helping finance the cost of animated projects. These artists all had an extensive, spirited range, often paying tribute to artists and illustrators of yesteryear. Channel 4, itself, could well be considered as pioneers in the computer-graphics field through making early use of CGI for their logo (1982), which consisted of multicolored shapes flying around the screen, finally forming the number four.

## Gifted Artists

Among the talents who sprang to light in this era was former teacher Sheila Graber (b.1940). She first decided to make animated films in 1970, but did not quite know how to go about it until she enlisted help from her local ciné club. With the success following from her films, Graber is now in a position to teach children every aspect of animation, "from Plasticine to pixels". Her trailblazing animated film *Heidi's Horse* (1987) pictures a child's artistic development.

Paul Vester had also been around since the 1970s, making unique use of cel animation in his musical cartoons such as *Football Freaks* (1971) and particularly *Sunbeam* (1980), in which he produced an animated version of a 1930s-style musical patterned after the early animated cartoons of that era.

The gifted Geoff Dunbar (b.1944), without any formal art training, began his career with Larkins studio in 1965 making advertising films. In 1968 he joined Halas & Bachelor, where he was made supervisor of a new commercials division. After a spell at Dragon Productions, he formed his own "Grand Slamm Animation" studio. He first caught the public's eye with his faithful representation of the paintings of Toulouse Lautrec with *Lautrec* (1974). The success of *Lautrec* was followed by Dunbar's interpretation of Alfred Jarry's anarchic nineteenth-century play *Ubu Roi* under the less complicated title of *Ubu* (1978). He has chalked up a number of awards along the way as well, having Paul McCartney's 'We All Sing Together' from *Rupert and the Frog Song* (1984) in the British top 10. Dunbar's latest project is the 58-minute film *The Cunning Little Vixen* (2003).

## A Variety of Animation

Richard Ollive was influenced by turn-of-the-nineteenth-century artists such as Aubrey Beardsley and Arthur Rackham when he made *Night Visitors* (1974). The story involves a policeman, on night beat, who comes across Peter Pan and other nocturnal fantasy characters.

### Face in Art

For over 20 years Sheila Graber has delighted audiences of all ages with her imaginative animated films about artists and art education. The films use a number of animation techniques in exploring the work of a certain artist as well as more general concepts in art.

### Mondrian

This is from Sheila Graber's 1978 film *Mondrian*. She uses animation to stimulate an interest in art.

© Sheila Graber

## Twentieth Century Face

Having been an art teacher for 20 years, encouraging her pupils to find their creative outlet in paint, clay, wood, metal and finally animation, Graber still believes that animation is the "art of the future".

Satirical cartoonist Gerald Scarfe has also been known to dabble in animation. He first put his foot into the water by illustrating the early pop video, Pink Floyd's 'The Wall' (1981), which was animated straight onto film, providing a memorable image of hammers marching along to knock down the wall.

Barry Purves started his career by animating puppets at the Cosgrove-Hall studios, and then moved to computer animation with his five three-minute spots made for Channel 4, *The Very Models*, based on the songs of Gilbert and Sullivan.

Scotland-based Lesley Keen expanded on the Swiss artist Paul Klee's observation that "drawing is no more than taking a line for a walk" in his computer-animated tribute *Taking a Line For a Walk* (1983).

David Anderson included his *Dreamless Sleep* (1986) as part of the Channel 4 series *Sweet Disasters*. The film features the animation of wax figures that await a mysterious event in an atmosphere of pensive anticipation.

A protégé of Richard Williams, Tony White (b.1954) was thrown in at the deep end when he first joined the team as Williams' assistant on *A Christmas Carol* (1971). He was then left to direct the credit sequence for *The Pink Panther Strikes Again* (1976) while Williams was out of the country. However, it was his visual interpretation of the Japanese artist Hokusai's paintings in *Hokusai: An Animated Sketchbook* (1978) that brought him independent fame. He has since written a book on animating, *Animator's Workbook* (1988) and more recently has concentrated his talents on computer animation.

# PANNONIA STUDIO

Hungarian animation reached new levels of international success in the 1980s. Pannonia was producing more films than ever before while winning international acclaim for their work. In 1981, Ferenc Rófusz's masterful short *The Fly* – about the killing of a fly from the fly's perspective – won the Oscar for Best Animated Short. A few months later, Pannonia won its third Golden Palm award for *Perpetual Motion* (about the incredible things that happen to a man each time he enters an elevator) by Béla Vajda.

## TV and Features

Television production also reached a new peak. Pannonia was producing, on average, five series per year, including *Pom-Pom* by Attila Dargay, *The Curious Elephanny* by Zsolt Richly, *Csepke* by Ferenc Varsányi, *Trumpy and the Fire Troll* by Tamás Baksa, and, from two newcomers, *Never Mind Toby* by Ferenc Cakó and *Augusta* by Csaba Varga,

During this period, Pannonia produced an incredible 20 animated features, including *The Son of White Mare* (1980) by Marcell Jankovics, which in 1984 was acknowledged in Los Angeles as one of the best animation films ever made. The film combines various art styles (including Art Deco and Art Nouveau) with popular legends. Other notable features included the box office success *Vuk* (1981) by Attila Dargay, *Heroic Times* (1982) by József Gémes, *John the Boaster* (1983) by Zsolt Richly, *Saffi* (1984) by Attila Dargay, *The Captain of The Forest* (1987) by Attila Dargay and *Willy The Sparrow* (1988) by József Gémes.

## Abundance of Talent

While veteran animators like Sándor Reisenbüchler of *Farewell Little Island* (1987) and István Orosz of *Ah, America!* (1984) continued to produce strong short films, the decade was dominated by a wealth of new talent who brought not only new ideas, but also a desire, perhaps encouraged by the Oscar success of *The Fly*, to try new animation techniques. Csaba Varga's *The Luncheon* (1980) used clay animation, Ferenc Cakó's *Ab*

**Vuk**

Attila Dargay's *Vuk* was first in an impressive list of successfu animated features made by Pannonia in the 1980s.

**Vuk – character outlines**

This was Hungary's second largest-ever box office hit. Als known as *The Little Fox*, it was concerned with a young fox whose family is killed by hunters and who is raised by his wise old uncle

© Pannonia Film

The Disney studio followed up *The Little Mermaid* with *The Rescuers Down Under* (1990), the first time Disney made an animated feature film sequel. But the sequel did not do as well critically or financially as *The Little Mermaid*.

### Award-Winning Animation

However, *Beauty and the Beast* (1991), directed by Kirk Wise and Gary Trousdale, was a massive hit. Once again, Howard Ashman and Alan Mencken provided the music, with Ashman also producing and contributing to the story. It was the first animated feature in history to be nominated for the Academy Award for Best Picture. *Aladdin* (1992), John Musker and Ron Clements' follow-up to *The Little Mermaid*, did even better at the box office. The character of the Genie, voiced by Robin Williams and animated by Eric Goldberg, stole the show.

*The Lion King* (1994), directed by Roger Allers and Rob Minkoff, set the record for the highest-grossing traditionally animated film. Loosely based on *Hamlet*, the film told the mythical story of a son having to avenge the death of his father. Ironically, the studio did not have high expectations for the film. They were convinced that

**Simba and Mufassa**

While most of *The Lion King* was hand-drawn, there were certain effects the director wanted that would be extremely time-consuming to draw by hand. The wildebeest stampede, for example, was based on a wildebeest from a character designer's hand-drawn artwork. A 3D-computer model was created and replicated in order to produce the stampede seen on the film.

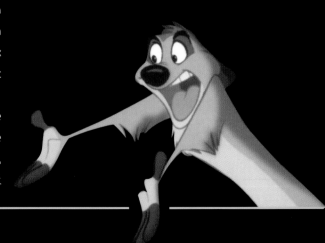

© The Walt Disney Company

## Pumbaa and Timon

Producing a hand-drawn animated film is extremely labor-intensive: more than 600 artists, animators and technicians contributed to *The Lion King* and more than a million drawings were created for it. It is made up of 1,197 hand-painted backgrounds and 119,058 individually colored frames of film.

## Simba and Scar

*The Lion King*'s working title was "King of the Jungle", and when production began on it, the artistic team traveled to Africa to research how best to portray the different locations on-screen. Lions and other animals were brought to the studio so the animators could study them.

© The Walt Disney Company

*Pocahontas* (1995) was the one that would be a blockbuster. *Pocahontas* did not do as well as *The Lion King* and was the start of a decline in the success of Disney animation.

## All Change

Several factors contributed to changes at the studio. Howard Ashman died during the production of *Aladdin*. The success of *Beauty and the Beast* and *The Lion King* caused other companies to start producing animated features. This diluted the talent pool and forced up wages and budgets. Because Disney animation represented such a large investment and potential profit, management interfered more in the making of the films.

Pretentiousness also crept into the Disney features. *Pocahontas* and *The Hunchback of Notre Dame* (1996) were films that seemed more interested in critical accolades than in entertaining audiences. The warmth that marked films like *The Little Mermaid* was in short supply in later films such as *Hercules* (1997), *Tarzan* (1999), *The Emperor's New Groove* (2000), *Atlantis* (2001) and *Treasure Planet* (2002).

To increase production, Disney opened up a satellite studio in Orlando, Florida. Perhaps because they were separated from Disney management by distance, the studio produced more successful films. *Mulan* (1998) followed the formula of earlier Disney successes, but followed it in an entertaining fashion. *Lilo and Stitch* (2002) attempted to duplicate the spirit of *Dumbo* and met with great box office success. *Brother Bear* (2003) was their swan song. While it had story problems, it attempted to grapple with larger themes than the typical Disney film and did better with audiences than the studio expected.

By 2004, Disney had closed the studio in Florida and drastically reduced the size of the California studio. Management decided to abandon drawn animation in favor of computer animation. Sadly *Home on the Range* (2004) marked the end of traditional Disney animation as practiced by Walt Disney.

# DIGITAL DOMAIN

When *Tron* was released in 1982, computer animation was still in its infancy. It cost over $20 million, and its lackluster box office gave Hollywood little incentive to invest in digital animation.

## Technology Not Ready

In some respects, that may have been a good decision. Computers of the time were relatively slow and very expensive, and there were very few artists who had the patience to put up with the difficult software available at the time. In the early 1980s, computer animation was simply not ready for prime-time.

The rest of the decade served as the industry's adolescence. The people involved in the CGI community had to figure out ways to turn the technology into a real business. Digital studios had to find ways to hit production deadlines and meet budgets that matched those of more traditional studios. As the decade progressed, the animation itself improved as more artists became involved, the software matured and workstations got faster and cheaper.

Most of the major digital studios got their start in the 1980s. Industrial Light and Magic (ILM) experimented with digital techniques throughout the decade, mostly in the area of editing, but also with feature-film effects. Pacific Data Images (PDI) was one of the first successful independent studios. Founded in 1980, the company found its early niche in the field of broadcast graphics. Pixar was founded in 1986, while 1987 saw the opening of Rhythm & Hues and Blue Sky.

## CGI Revolution

The large studios were also dabbling in digital. In 1986, Disney made its first use of computer graphics in the film *The Great Mouse Detective*. In this pioneering attempt, they used a computer to calculate and draw the inside of a clock for the final chase sequence. Subsequently, the studio began using other digital techniques on traditionally animated films.

By the end of the decade, the talent and tools were in place for digital animation to take a leading role in Hollywood. The first big splash came from ILM with an effect for an underwater movie called *The Abyss* (1989). ILM created a creature made of water that interacted with the live-action

### Jurassic Park

The dinosaurs were created using a mixture of digital animation and animatronics. As a general rule, if the dinosaur was shown in full, then it had been rendered digitally, while shots of the dinosaurs' body parts were of animatronics.

### Drawing from Jurassic Park

The digital technology used in *Jurassic Park* was able, for the first time, to create realistic, living, breathing characters with skin, muscles and texture. This breakthrough expanded the film-maker's canvas and changed the cinematic art of storytelling.

### Terminator 2

In this film, the T-1000 changes from one form to another via a computer process known as morphing. This involves taking two images or series of images and finding similarities between the pixels or shape of one and the pixels or shape of another. Recognizable structures are often shaped or changed from one image to another, while other parts are blurred or their color palettes reduced so one image or one pixel can become the same as the other.

© Artisan Entertainment

actors. This sequence demonstrated a new level of realism and showed just how far CGI had come. The success of *The Abyss* gave ILM the courage to attempt bigger digital projects.

ILM scored another big success in 1991 with *Terminator 2: Judgment Day*. This film contained dozens of digital effects, including a digital representation of Robert Patrick as the liquid metal T-1000. The next huge leap forward was *Jurassic Park*. The dinosaurs in the film proved CGI could compete against traditional animation and effects, and in many ways with better results.

A revolution was under way in Hollywood. The maturing of CGI in the early 1990s changed the way traditional live-action movies were made. It was also about to revolutionize the process of creating animated films.

# PIXAR & TOY STORY

By 1991, Pixar was one of the leading computer-animation studios and very confident in its production methods. That year, Disney announced an agreement with Pixar to create the first computer-animated full-length feature film: *Toy Story* (1995). For many of the people at the studio this was a dream come true, a dream that had started 20 years earlier in the quiet of the university research labs.

## In the Making

*Toy Story* was the moment when computer animation became a true force in Hollywood. Just as *Snow White* was the point where traditional animation matured into a true art form, *Toy Story* was the point where computer animation truly came of age. Since its release, computer-animated films have taken Hollywood by storm.

*Toy Story* took almost four years to make. Until 1991, when Disney gave them the financing to create a full-length feature film, Pixar had only produced a few short films and a string of 30-second commercials. Creating almost an hour and a half of quality feature footage was a very high mark to hit, and they had to devise a new way of making movies on computers.

Pixar pitched a story to Disney about something they knew – toys. This subject was chosen partly on the success of *Tin Toy*, and partly because Pixar knew that toys could be animated much more realistically than other types of characters with the technology available. The story was a classic "buddy" picture exploring the tenuous relationship between cowboy Woody and space cadet Buzz Lightyear, whose arrival threatens Woody's position as Andy's favorite toy. The two heroes hit it off poorly, but finally find a way to work together when they land in the hands of Sid, a demented kid with a taste for explosives.

The story process for *Toy Story* was the same as for any animated feature, with a script, hand-drawn storyboards and plenty of conceptual art. It went through a number of revisions and, after almost 18 months, was ready for production.

## Teamwork

While the story was taking shape, Pixar employed large numbers of new staff for the film. The animators' backgrounds were largely in traditional cel and stop-motion animation; other traditional artists were hired to paint textures and provide lighting. In addition, the studio engaged an equally large team of computer scientists and engineers to assist with the technical side of things.

Pixar developed an animation pipeline that bridged the unique talents of artists, scientists and engineers. Artists focused on making the movie look good, while the technical staff backed them up by managing the computers and writing custom software to help the artists realize their visions.

### Buzz Lightyear

In order to make their characters' movements look realistic, the animators looked at what the toys were made of: Buzz was rigid, and his ball-and-socket joints gave him a purposeful stride; Woody was a floppy, loose, limp rag doll.

### Toy Story

With *Toy Story*, Pixar formulated the technique of constructing characters as a series of digital models with limbs and facial expressions that could then be moved in any direction inside the computer environment. The result was that the animation camera could track and move through the CG action in almost exactly the same way that a tracking shot could do with live-action.

### Woody

After completing the characters' body animations, the animators created the facial animation and lip sync. To create the facial animation, each main character was modeled with "pull points" for facial muscles. The animator-performer could pull down Woody's forehead into a frown – he had eight controls for his eyebrows alone.

Pixar and *Tin Toy* » 270

© Pixar Animation Studios, Walt Disney Studios

## Character Creation

Many of the tasks, such as art direction, were done by hand. Special care was taken to give the environments a stylized storybook look. Instead of the painted backgrounds used in most animated films, Pixar created 3D-digital sets, modeled by artists and technicians. The sets were then textured, using paintings as well as photographs to give the film a realistic yet "cartoony" feel.

Characters were first created on paper, then sculpted in clay and digitized into the computer. A team of computer-savvy technical directors then "wired" the digital characters with virtual controls for the animators to manipulate. An animator might have several dozen controls for creating facial expressions, for example.

Animating 3D characters on a computer is different from other types of animation. Animators pose their characters much like real-world puppets, but through the flat screen of a computer. Unlike stop-motion, however, the animators have the ability to finesse the animation as much as they want, giving supersmooth and controllable results.

## The Final Result

The animation was then passed off to a lighting and rendering team, who brought the final product to the screen. Sets and characters were lit with digital lights much like in any live-action feature, and the resulting frames were rendered on a bank of several hundred computers into a final film.

Despite all the technical hurdles Pixar had to endure during its creation, they managed to create a film with great characters and an engaging story. *Toy Story* was the top animated hit of 1995. It was the first of a string of successes Pixar would rack up over the next few years, putting traditionally animated features on the defensive and making digitally animated features the new rage in Hollywood.

# FEATURE PLAYERS

In August 1994, two months after the opening of Disney's hugely successful *The Lion King*, Jeffrey Katzenberg, Steven Spielberg and David Geffen formed DreamWorks SKG. From the very start, the new company had instant credibility in terms of animation; after all, Katzenberg had been a key figure in the revival of Disney's animation fortunes, and Spielberg had been involved in such groundbreaking films as *An American Tail* and *Who Framed Roger Rabbit?*.

## Competing with Disney

DreamWorks' formation followed closely on moves by Warner Bros. and Twentieth Century Fox to set up their own feature animation divisions. All three aimed to compete head-on with Disney in producing big-budget animation blockbusters, a field the "mouse house" had had all to itself since Don Bluth's arrangement with Spielberg fell apart.

## Warner Bros.

Warner's first animated feature in the new gold rush was the live-action/animated *Space Jam* (1996). Inspired by the Air Jordan TV commercials, it featured Michael Jordan and the classic *Looney Tunes* characters. Though often overwrought, it proved both popular and profitable. The unit's first all-animated effort, Frederik Du Chau's *Quest for Camelot* (1998), proved to be a rather inept Arthurian romance.

However, this was followed by Brad Bird's wonderful *The Iron Giant* (1999), based on Ted Hughes' book about a boy who befriends a robot from outer space. Although widely acclaimed by critics and animators alike, it failed at the box office. *Looney Tunes: Back in Action* (2003), by Joe Dante and Eric Goldberg, a surprisingly good follow-up to *Space Jam*, also failed to capture the public's attention.

## Twentieth Century Fox

For the new Fox Animation Studios in Phoenix, Arizona, Don Bluth and Gary Goldman were brought in from Ireland as producers. Their first effort was *Anastasia* (1997), a smartly done musical remake of Anatole Litvak's 1956 movie, which seemed to herald a comeback for Bluth. However, *Bartok the Magnificent* (1999), the film's direct-to-video prequel, and *Titan A.E.* (2000), a poorly received sci-fi adventure blending cel and CG animation, spelled the end of the Phoenix operation. Fox instead shifted from traditional cel animation to CGI, and specifically to its newly acquired Blue Sky Studios, a company that traced its pedigree to MAGI SynthaVision, one of the two companies that did the computer animation for Disney's *Tron*. The result was Chris Wedge's *Ice Age* (2002), a hilarious takeoff of Peter B. Kyne's often-filmed book *The Three Godfathers*. Particularly striking were the stylized character designs by famed illustrator Peter DeSève, which dramatically broke away from the Pixar-style realism that had previously dominated computer-animated movies.

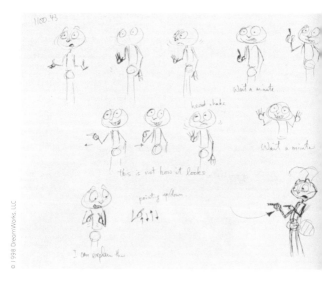

© 1998 DreamWorks LLC

**Antz – model sheet**

PDI devised new facial-animation tools to create detailed expressions for Z and his fellow colony members based on an anatomical model of a face. Animators used combinations of controls that could raise an eyebrow, widen the eyes or dilate the pupils. There was also a less-detailed system that used shape interpolation and deformations rather than direct muscle control to animate faces.

**Antz – crowd**

*Antz*'s animators needed to animate everything from a small group of background characters to thousands of ants in a battle scene. The technical directors created two types of crowd systems: the first was used for groups of fewer than 50 ants, which blended a mixture of body types and motions; and the second was used for larger crowds, which gave animators less control and more automation.

**Z and Weaver**

*Antz*'s characters, with their organic body shapes and expressive faces, were a breakthrough in CG film. The facial animation system developed by PDI paid great attention to detail, and in particular offered a lot of eye control. For instance, when an eyeball turned, it actually grabbed the eyelid. Instances such as this added greater depth to the film.

Don Bluth » 274  DreamWorks » 344  Blue Sky & *Ice Age* » 346

© Aardman Ltd. 1989

## Creature Comforts

This Oscar-winning short from 1989 by Nick Park was part of the Aardman series *Lip Synch*. It was a critical and popular success, and inspired a celebrated advertising campaign in which Claymation animals acted as spokepersons for an electricity board.

## Morph

Created by Peter Lord and David Sproxton in 1976, Morph brought Claymation into the homes of millions for the first time. Although Morph's first appearances were only one-minute segments in a children's TV show, he was such an original and dynamic figure that he soon became the star attraction. He was the start of a re-invigoration of animation in Britain.

(1970). This initial effort was purchased by the BBC for use in the television program *Vision On*, an innovative art presentation for deaf children fronted by the talented artist Tony Hart. When the $45 (£25) for their efforts arrived from the BBC, the bank wanted to know the name of their company account and, for want of a better title, they blurted out it was "Aardman Animations".

## It All Started with Morph

Not content with the expense and trouble of making hand-drawn cel animation or cut-outs, the boys decided to create a Plasticine world by using clay models that could be altered and reused with the minimum of cost. They continued contributing to *Vision On* while resuming their respective educations at separate universities. Soon, with their college days behind them, the two decided to pursue a career in animation and contacted the BBC again. Unfortunately, *Vision On*'s days were over, but a similar program, *Take Hart*, was just being instigated, and its producer wanted something that was "alive" on presenter Tony Hart's desktop for him to respond to.

Thus was born "Morph", an orange anthropomorphic Plasticine character with a symmetrical head, rubbery arms and legs and big feet who first appeared on the *Take Hart* tabletop in 1978. The simple plot line would follow Morph, always eager to help Tony with his art and, more often than not, messing it up and having to return to his box.

## Short Conversations

In 1978 Lord and Sproxton took a risk with their *Animated Conversations*, structured around random conversations secretly recorded at a Salvation Army shelter and putting the dialogue into the mouths of their clay characters. *The Animated Conversations – Confessions of a Foyer Girl* and *Down and Out* proved successful and brought international recognition for them both. Leading on from this, a further series of five shorts titled *Conversation Pieces* were commissioned for Channel 4. For a while Aardman's stock-in-trade was the *Animated Conversations* theme of using unscripted conversations discussing the mundane happenings in daily life, expressed only by the Plasticine faces.

# CLAY MAKES HAY

Aardman's finest hour came in 1982 with the arrival of a brand-new television channel, Channel 4 which, at the outset, was keen to commission and encourage young animators to make fresh films for their own consumption. Aardman suggested more *Conversation Pieces*, namely *Lip Synch*, which ultimately spiraled into Nick Park's (b. 1958) *Creature Comforts* which won an Oscar for the best Animated Short Film of 1990.

## The Start of a Good Thing

The essence of *Creature Comforts* is caged animals in an English zoo expressing their opinions on the state of the world, with voices supplied by putting casual vox populi interviews to extremely good use. Once Channel 4 got rolling, the

© Aardman/Wallace & Gromit Ltd 1993

work for Aardman started flooding in: pop videos embracing the likes of Peter Gabriel, along with a plethora of commercials for such products as Scotch videotape, Cadbury's Cream Eggs, Angel Delight, British Gas and Lurpak butter.

## Introducing Wallace and Gromit

The year 1985 hailed the arrival of Nick Park, who brought with him a film he had started as a student at the National Film and Television School. This was to be the half-hour legend *A Grand Day Out* (1989) introducing the cracking-good combination of inventor Wallace (perfectly voiced by actor Peter Sallis) and his astute sidekick, Gromit. In their debut, Wallace being more than moderately fond of cheese, they build a rocket ship in the expectation of finding cheese on the moon. Park, his work easily identified by characters with "coat hanger mouths", spent six years working on this project, finally completing the film after joining Aardman. It scored a direct hit with the end result earning an Academy Award nomination.

After Nick Park's *A Grand Day Out* was acquired by the BBC, it was decided that a sequel would be in order. The second short film turned out to be the epic adventure *The Wrong Trousers* (1993), which involved the lethal combination of Wallace's

### The Wrong Trousers

In order to synchronize Wallace's lip and face movements to the recording made of Wallace's voice by actor Peter Sallis, Nick Park worked with "dope sheets", which broke down the speech into phonetics on a frame-by-frame basis. This allowed him to know exactly what sound was being made by the character at any point in the shot.

### A Close Shave

This short, as with the previous ones, was treated like a live-action drama. Everything was designed and built around the camera in order to keep it visually interesting and to maintain a filmic look, rather than just building a set and filming on it.

© Kratky Film

### The Little Mole

Kratky Film's series *The Little Mole*, 70 percent funded by a German broadcaster, is an example of one of the international series currently being made in the formerly state-run studios of Eastern Europe.

© Kratky Film

gigantic dog, designed by another great Czech illustrator, Jiri Salamoun, and directed by Vaclav Bedrich. Probably the best-known animated films produced at the Prague studio are dozens of shorts starring the Little Mole, based on books by Zdenek Miler. The studio has also recently received commissions from the Czech Ministry of Education, including one on stress by Milan Klikar.

## Reputation to Uphold

Founded in 1945, Bratri v Triku has an illustrious history to live up to. Jiri Trnka was one of its founders, along with other Czech masters like Bretislav Pojar, Jiri Brdecka and Zdenek Miler. The studio currently employs 35 full-time animators, with another 35 or so regular freelancers, who produce more than 200 minutes of animation each year.

# ANIME IN THE 1990s

By the 1990s, there were accusations that Japanese animation had become creatively bankrupt. There were no new concepts — just variations on worn-out themes and remakes of past hits. Despite this complaint, the popularity of animation grew to new global proportions.

## New Creativity Emerges

Leading feature directors of the decade (besides Miyazaki and Takahata) include Mamoru Oshii, Yoshiaki Kawajiri, Rintaro, Satoshi Kon, Takashi Nakamura, Hiroyuki Okiura and Hiroyuki Kitakubo. Oshii stands out, not only for the features he directed, including *Patlabor: The Movie* (1990), *Patlabor 2* (1993) and *Ghost in the Shell* (1995), but for overseeing the creative teams that would produce cutting-edge animation features *Jin-Roh: The Wolf Brigade* (1999), directed by Okiura, and *Blood: The Last Vampire* (2000), directed by Kitakubo.

*Ghost*, *Jin-Roh* and *Blood* were productions of Production I.G, one of the more prominent new animation studios of this decade — co-founded in 1987 by character designer Takayuki Goto and Mitsuhisa Ishikawa (b. 1958).

The Madhouse studio, and its distinctive character designer/director Yoshiaki Kawajiri, established a trademark style of adult situations featuring characters who are sophisticated, sensual and dangerous. Kawajiri's *Ninja Scroll* (1993) made his often-delayed *Vampire Hunter D: Bloodlust* (2001) eagerly anticipated throughout the 1990s. Madhouse was also responsible for the critically acclaimed features of Satoshi Kon, starting with *Perfect Blue* (1997). Also of note is *Catnapped!* (1995) — a witty and visually imaginative children's film directed by Takashi Nakamura.

## For Boys and Girls

Millions around the world who had never heard of Japanese animation learned of it in the 1990s because of international headlines in December 1997 that claimed a strobing-light effect in an episode of *Pocket Monsters* (a.k.a. *Pokémon*) had given "up to 12,000" children epileptic fits.

For boys, TV animation continued to be dominated by *Dragon Ball* and its *Dragon Ball Z* (1989–96) and *Dragon Ball GT* (1996–97) sequels. Also extremely popular were programs spun off from popular video games featuring young heroes who befriend cute fantasy animals with special powers. *Pokémon*, a 1997 TV series based upon a 1996 video game with 151 pocket-size "monsters", established itself as a worldwide fad. *Digimon* (1999) and *Monster Rancher* (1999) have been the most popular of its imitators. *Detective Conan* (a.k.a. *Case Closed*, 1996) presented a skilled

### Princess Mononoke

This 1997 feature was a tour de force. Hayao Miyazaki and his team created a primeval forest where the gods still rule and the life force of the forest is intact, manifested in the presence of forest sprites. The rich, dark greens and the delicately drawn texture of the trees, moss, rocks, and water surfaces create a world as realistic as any live-action setting.

© Miramax Films

### The Sandwiches

Yamamura's 1993 short won various prizes at festivals, including Chicago International Children's Festival and World Youth Film Festival.

### The Sandwiches – work in progress

Koji Yamamura eschews the assembly-line approach to animation, and prefers working alone. His pieces contain few words, and he uses pencils, markers, clay or a combination of several materials. *The Sandwiches* was created with clay, puppets, photos and drawings on cel.

**Pokémon**

After the success of the TV series, *Pokémon: The First Movie* was released in 1998, and a second in 2000 (pictured). The success of the franchise has been perpetuated by further films, and parents continue to be pestered by their children for the spin-off cards and games as the merchandising continues unabated.

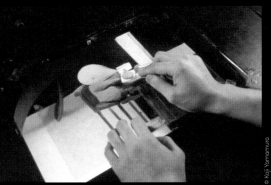

detective who is physically transformed into a seven-year-old boy and uses this handicap as an excellent disguise. For younger girls, the decade's most popular TV series were *Sailor Moon* (1992) and *Card Captor Sakura* (1998). *Sailor Moon*'s original director, Kunihiko Ikuhara (b. 1964), went on to guide the more surrealistic schoolgirl fantasy *Revolutionary Girl Utena* (1997), set in a vast ethereal high school.

Other notable TV animation included *Neon Genesis Evangelion* (1995), a giant robot drama that evolved in darkly psychological directions. *Evangelion* and the earlier *Nadia: The Secret of Blue Water* (1990) helped establish the Gainax studio's reputation for imaginative TV animation. Sophisticated adults swung to *Cowboy Bebop* (1998), a jazzy meld of futuristic space opera, noir private investigator drama, cynical comedy, hand-drawn and cel animation, and in-group references to the favorite cinematic influences of director Shinichiro Watanabe (b. 1965).

*Serial Experiments Lain* (1998), a sci-fi drama about the nature of reality, demonstrated how imaginative direction, by Ryutaro Nakamura; intelligent writing, by Chiaki Konaka (b.1961); and experimental art design, by Yoshitoshi Abe (b. 1971), could make what was clearly a low-budget TV series tense and gripping.

## OAVs: From Medieval Fantasy to High-Tech

Highlights included *Record of Lodoss War* (1990), which introduced heroic sword and sorcery fantasy to animation, with humans, elves and dwarves fighting evil in a medieval Europe, and the comedy-adventure *Slayers* (1995) featuring tomboy sorceress Lina Inverse. Director/character designer Hiroyuki Ochi made the 1995 four-episode *Armitage III: Poly-Matrix* as an imaginative tribute to the sci-fi cyber-technology themes of Philip K. Dick, with enough flair and quality that the OAV series was released internationally as a theatrical feature.

Shoji Kawamori (b. 1958) proved equally adept at various genres, directing the sci-fi sequel *Macross Plus* (1995); directing the hauntingly surrealistic biography of author Kenji Miyazawa, *Spring and Chaos* (1996); and plotting the hit TV series *The Vision of Escaflowne* (1996), an adventure-romance of a Japanese high school girl who is transported to a fantasy world. Computer graphics appeared even more spectacularly in the OAV sci-fi series *Blue Submarine No. 6* (1998), the first that the public saw of new CGI-intensive Studio Gonzo (founded 1993) and its director Mahiro Maeda (b. 1963).

In the film festival world, Koji Yamamura (b. 1964) emerged as a major new talent of the 1990s, averaging one new film per year. His prizewinning films include *The Elevator* (1991); *A House* (1993), *The Sandwiches* (1993) and *Imagination* (1993), all featuring his characters Karo and Piyobupt; *Bavel's Book* (1996); and *Your Choice!* (1999). His Yamamura Animation, Inc. (founded 1993) also produces TV commercials.

# ASIA ARISES

The 1990s was a time of great turmoil for South Korean animation, which saw a major decline in overseas work and the introduction of major government initiatives to revitalize the industry.

## Supporting the Industry

The worldwide boom in TV production collapsed amid a trend towards consolidation among US producers, distributors and broadcasters, aggravated by the Asian currency crisis. The decline was accelerated by the growing popularity of Japanese animation in the wake of the *Pokémon* phenomenon. As a result, Western producers began to shift production to lower-cost areas like China; while some Korean studios managed to retain contracts for high-profile shows like *The Simpsons* and *Futurama*, most were forced to enter into co-production deals that lowered their profit margins.

It soon became clear that the only way the industry could survive would be through development of original productions, but the long-standing emphasis on service work had left it without the experience to produce work of international appeal by themselves. This is a problem that has also affected other Pacific Rim countries. Even Tooniverse, the cartoon channel established in 1994, has been unable to meet its goal of 70 percent domestic programming.

## Awards and Festivals

In 1995, for the first time, the government provided tax incentives to spur production, established the Seoul International Cartoon and Animation Festival (SICAF) and Korean Animated Film Awards, and fostered the growth of animation training. This led to greater investment in animation by larger corporations, including some *chaebols* ("conglomerates"). A new boom in feature animation followed. These included *Blue Seagull* (1994), Korea's first adult animated feature, which was a popular if not a critical success; *The Return of Hong Gil Dong* (1995), a Japanese-style remake of Shin Dong Hun's pioneering effort; and *Little*

### The Return of Hong Gil Dong

This film was a remake of *Hong Gil Dong*, the first Korean animation made for theaters and released in 1967. Although it told the same story as its predecessor, the influence of Japanese anime could clearly be seen in its artwork.

### Poster

The first Seoul International Cartoon and Animation Festival (SICAF) was held in 1995. It aimed to elevate exposure to animation with its screenings and exhibitions of 2,500 works from 37 countries. It was a great success, and the festival is now the most popular in Asia.

### Blue Seagull

This was South Korea's first adult animated feature, and was a huge box office success, despite criticism for its low-quality production and sexual imagery.

Courtesy of John A. Lent

Courtesy of John A. Lent

*Dinosaur Dooly* (1996), based on the popular comic strip, which gained some international distribution. These and other films, though, were criticized for their lack of technical proficiency, forcing producers to start collaborating with Japanese studios.

In recent years, Korean TV animation has had some success in Asian markets, especially in China, although some of these efforts have been derided as *Pokémon* knockoffs. The Japanese influence is seen in Aitaska Studio's stop-motion fairy tale *Doggy Poo*, a Tokyo International Anime Fair award winner in 2003. Another series aimed at the international market was Grimi Production's *Ki-Fighter Taerang* (2001), a martial-arts/sci-fi adventure.

## Distinctive Style

In 2003, much hope was placed on the large-budgeted, futuristic dramatic feature *Wonderful Days*, directed by Kim Mun-saeng for Teen House; however, it was criticized because its beautiful visuals do not compensate for its weak plot and it failed at the box office. Another feature of note is Sung Baek-youb's *Oseam* (2003), "a fairy tale for adults" based on a novel by Jung Chae-bong and praised for its "delicate, watercolor look".

The most critically acclaimed animated movie of late has been Lee Sung-gang's *My Beautiful Girl, Mari* (2002), which won the Grand Prix at the Annecy International Animation Festival; filled with nostalgia, it tells how a boy uses his daydreams of a beautiful girl to get through some real-life personal crises. Though exhibiting some Japanese influence, it was praised for its distinctive Korean styling.

# ANINMATION FROM OTHER NATIONS

## Taiwan

Animation in Taiwan began with the production of short films in the 1960s by Tse-Hsiu Art and Production and Ying-Jen Ads Company. However, it was soon dominated by Wang Film Production Co., a.k.a. Cuckoo's Nest, established by the US-trained James Wang in 1978 in partnership with Hanna-Barbera. It soon became a dominant force in overseas animation and its credits include such TV shows as *Yogi Bear*, *Scooby-Doo* and *Garfield*, as well as features like *The Care Bears Movie*, *The Brave Little Toaster* and *Jetsons: The Movie*.

As labor costs escalated, Wang set up satellite studios in China and Thailand, a policy followed by other Taiwanese studios. At the same time, there were sporadic attempts at original productions, such as Wang's feature-length *Uncle Niou's Great Adventure* (1982). More recently veteran Tsai Ming-chin directed *Butterfly Lovers* (2003), based on China's famous tragic romance, for China's Shanghai Animation Film Studio.

In 2003, the government announced plans to reinvigorate local film and TV production and encourage co-productions with international partners, with special emphasis on digital production and animation, but it is too early to see any results from this initiative.

© Wang Film Production Co.

**Characters – Wang Film Production Co.**

James Wang's Taiwanese studio collaborates with animation companies worldwide, as well as producing its own material. Nearly half of all cartoons on US television credit Wang Film Production. Pictured are characters from some of his own films.

## Thailand

The father of Thai animation is Payut Ngaokrachang (b. 1929), whose first film was *The Miracle Incident* (1955), a 16 mm cartoon about a massive car pile-up, brought about when a beautiful woman walks by. This was followed by two anti-Communist films, *The New Adventures of Hanuman* (1958), for the United States Information Service based on a story in the *Ramayana*, and *A Child and a Bear* (1960), for SEATO. After making Thailand's first animated feature, *The Adventure of Sud Sakorn* (1979), Payut spent much of the 1990s teaching animation and made *My Way*, an anti-AIDS film, for the Japan Information Center.

Until recently, aside from Payut, animation in Thailand was dominated by offshore studios,

Courtesy Payut Ngaokrachang

Courtesy Payut Ngaokrachang

with sporadic attempts to develop domestic production, including the first local TV series, Kantana Animation's *Twin Witches*. Since the domestic market is not broad enough, there has been a push to make shows with broader appeal, with Cartooniverse Co. proclaiming its *Ray-Mimi Reaching the Star* (2003) the first Thai TV series made for an international audience.

**The New Adventures of Hanuman**

This short, made Payut Ngaokrachang, retells the classic tale of the white monkey from the *Ramayana*. Intended as anti-Communist propaganda, the propaganda element was present in the form of the red monkey, which represented Communism.

Indian Animation » 374

### The Adventure of Sud Sakorn

The production of Thailand's first animated feature was hampered by shortages of personnel, capital and equipment. Ngaokrachang made a lot of his own equipment from World War Two military surplus, and even adapted a combat camera.

### Poster

Australian company Energee Entertainment promotes Vietnamese animation. Growth in the animation industry is a result of investment from Western companies such as this, as well as an all-around growth in the international animation industry, whose executives recognize Vietnam as a good location in which to open low-cost facilities.

Beautiful Oriental fables from Vietnam teach children the true value of friendship and love. Timeless classics told using a variety of traditional animation techniques including drawings, papercut and 3D clay modelling. These delightful and provocative stories are available for the first time since Vietnam opened its doors to the western world.

## The Philippines

Animation in the Philippines has largely been dependent on work for foreign producers, though some indigenous production emerged around 1953 with occasional independent shorts and TV commercials. The year 1979 saw the release of *The Life of Lam-ang*, a feature by the American-trained Nonoy Marcelo, whose story deals with the birthplace of then President Ferdinand Marcos,

It was under Marcos that foreign studios began establishing overseas facilities with Australia's Burbank in 1983, followed by Fil-Cartoons (originally owned by Hanna-Barbera) and Philippine Animation Studio, Inc. (PASI), which worked on a variety of TV shows from *Johnny Bravo* to *DragonBall Z*. The legacy of American colonialism, with a population fluent in English, would seem to have given the Philippines an inherent advantage over other Asian countries; but due to poor management and other factors, this promise was never fulfilled. However, Philippine animators have frequently found work in North American studios, including major movies such as *Anastasia*.

Local production, outside of independent films, remains sporadic at best. The only TV series made in the Philippines, *Ang Panday* (1987), failed to get an audience, as did the feature-length *The Adarna Bird* (1997).

## Vietnam

Animation in Vietnam goes back to 1959, when the North Vietnamese Ministry of Culture founded the Hanoi Cartoon Studio. Over the years, it made short films using traditional cel, puppet and cut-out animation. Their first film was *What the Fox Deserves* (1960), a propaganda short by the Soviet-trained Le Minh Hien and Truong Qua. Their first film to gain international recognition was *The Kitty* by Ngo Manh Lan, which won an award at the 1966 Mamaia (Romania) Animation Festival and tells of a kitten who successfully organizes against an invading army of rats. Also highly praised was Truong Qua's *The Legend of the Region* (1977).

While the propaganda films have attracted the most attention, the majority of the studio's films were basically moralistic fables mostly using cut-out animation, such as Bui Ngo's *The Clumsy Bear*. Though this and other similar films are not without charm, they are nevertheless often lackluster in execution.

Beginning in 1991, Western companies started establishing overseas studios in Vietnam. Although the Hanoi Cartoon Studio is itself involved with this movement, most of these facilities have been established in Ho Chi Minh City, including Pixi Vietnam, a computer-animation studio that has worked on Nelvana's popular *Rolie Polie Olie* series.

# THE
# NEW CENTURY

As we begin a new millennium, animation art enters an era of change – a new phase of popular acceptance – and has artists redefining themselves.

Computer animation has taken over Hollywood. Due to the success of numerous CG cartoon features (*Finding Nemo, Ice Age, Shrek*), Hollywood studios have abandoned traditional hand-drawn techniques, Disney has down-sized, and Pixar has triumphed.

Hollywood has utilized the CG techniques to aid its live-action agenda – now many impossible situations (think *Titanic, The Matrix* and *Lord of the Rings*) are easier to accomplish. New hybrid movies integrating "cartoon" stars into live-action (*Garfield, Scooby-Doo* and *Rocky & Bullwinkle*) have found supersized success at the box office.

New techniques, derived from computer graphics, have provided pioneer opportunities: low-cost Flash animation has made TV-animation production more economical, while upscale motion capture technology (*The Polar Express*) has allowed animated actors to emote realistically.

And yet hand-drawn cartoons have not completely disappeared. Anime has sustained its worldwide grasp, as Japan's TV programs get more stylized and its theatrical features become more elaborate. Hayao Miyazaki's *Spirited Away* and Sylvain Chomet's *The Triplets of Belleville* have garnered global acclaim – and *The Simpsons* just keeps on going.

Animation Art is alive and well – and here to stay!

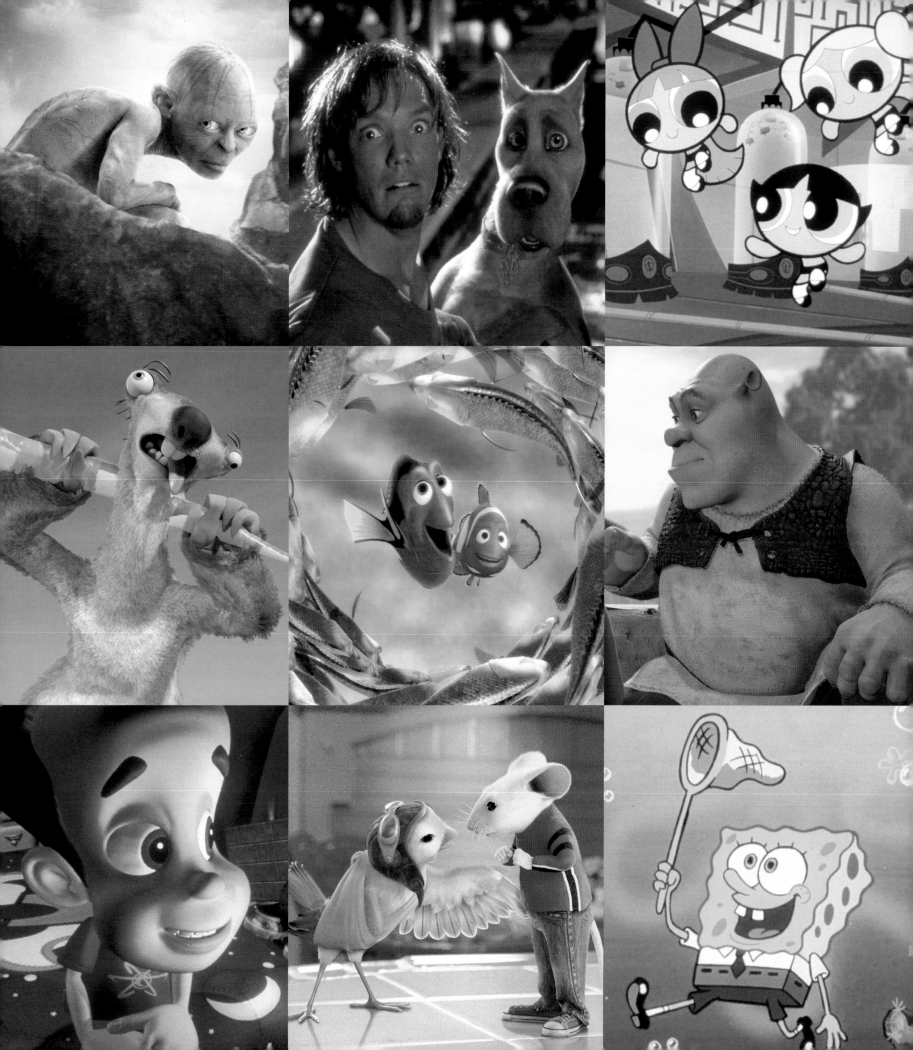

# CGI VICTORIOUS

A little over five years after the release of *Toy Story*, CGI animated features were dominating the box office. Films like *Shrek*, *Monsters, Inc.* (2001) and *Ice Age* proved to be wildly successful with audiences, setting box office records and leaving traditionally animated films in the dust. While some cel-animated films, such as *Lilo & Stitch* did quite well, they were the exception rather than the rule. In a very short amount of time, CGI went from being the exception to being the rule.

## Going Digital

This sudden change of fortune caused traditional animation studios to rethink their production methods. In 2003, after a string of mediocre box-office returns, Disney announced they were going digital for all future animated productions, ending almost 65 years of traditional cel animation at the studio. DreamWorks, though a much younger studio, made a similar decision at about the same time. While this was by no means the end of cel animation, the light table had certainly lost the position of dominance it once had.

### Fiona and Shrek

*Shrek* signaled a major advance in CG technology. For example, the animators managed to create realistic-looking clothing with fabric that wrinkled and moved as it would in real life, such as Fiona's velvet dress and Shrek's rough tunic. They were also able to "grow" forests with millions of leaves that would rustle in the breeze.

### Ice Age

Sid the Sloth started life on an artist's drawing board. From the initial pencil sketches, a 3D-clay model was created and then transferred to a computer. To do this, a grid was created on the model to allow the computer to recognize Sid's shape by recording the intersections of the lines. From those points of intersection the computer generated hundreds of curves, forming Sid's basic outline.

© 2002 20th Century Fox

## Stuart Little 2

The wireframe model used to create Stuart's face was extremely mobile, having been divided and subdivided into independently moveable parts. This allowed the animators maximum flexibility in choosing facial gestures and expressions. By animating more aspects of Stuart's facial gestures, more believable expressions were achieved.

© Columbia Pictures

While the visual novelty of CGI features was certainly a factor in this sudden change, these films also told a different type of story. Pixar avoided the cliché of the musical fairy tale, while *Shrek* simply slapped it in the face. These films had a very broad appeal, with complex characters, fewer formulas and plenty of jokes aimed directly at adults. They could be enjoyed by everyone, not just children, and were really good films. Hollywood put its money on these emerging studios and thereby attracted the best veteran artists and top young talent.

## Digital Domination

Digital characters were not only dominating animated features, they also were taking big roles in live-action films as well. During the 1990s, digital characters went from being one-dimensional monsters to fully integrated cast members. Films such as *Stuart Little* (1999) and *Star Wars: Episode I – The Phantom Menace* (1999) featured digital characters in starring roles.

This overlap started to blur the line between live-action and animation. How should films such as *Stuart Little*, which stars a computer-animated mouse in the title role, be defined? Is it a live-action film or an animated one? This question became even more relevant as an Academy Award was created for Best Animated Feature. The first of these Oscars was given to *Shrek* in 2002, showing just how far the art form had come in a few years.

Digital techniques have completely changed the landscape of Hollywood film-making within the span of a decade. Animation, once relegated to Termite Terraces on the studio back lot, was now part of the mainstream. The landscape has been permanently changed, and, thanks to the innovations of CGI, animation is hotter than ever.

# MONSTERS, INC.

*Monsters, Inc.* was the film in which Pixar mastered the art of digital film-making, and its release marked the point where the studio became the hippest in Hollywood. It was visually stunning and the animation appeared effortless.

## Scary Monsters

The film concerns Sulley (John Goodman) who, with the help of his partner Mike (Billy Crystal), is the top scarer at Monsters, Inc. Sulley's job is to scare small children so that their screams can be turned into electricity to power Monstropolis. Sulley's nemesis is the chameleon-like Randall Boggs (Steve Buscemi), who desperately wants to unseat Sulley as the top scarer.

## Realistic and Believable

It was thanks to the visuals that the film shone. Its main set was a 100-year-old factory town, complete with dirt and grime. In addition to the town, Pixar designed a winter scene complete with realistic snow. The character design in the film was excellent. Unlike

### Monsters, Inc.

Until the development of Fizt, realistic animation of certain effects — hair blowing in the wind or a shirt wrinkling with its wearer — was practically impossible to achieve. As well as simulating the movements of fur, clothing, and other materials, Fizt made it possible to portray a wide variety of emotions in animated characters by enhancing facial expressions and the realism of body language.

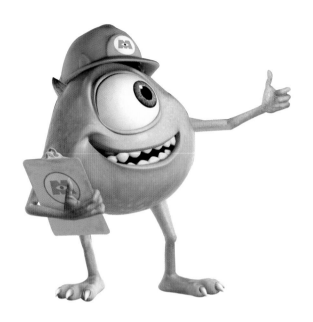

## Monsters, Inc. Characters

The success of *Monsters, Inc.* was partly due to the very imaginative range of characters. The animation leads were faced with new challenges of how to achieve realistic facial expressions and body language with one eye or several crustacean legs. Sulley's 2,320,413 computer-animated hairs were created and controlled using several programmes including a RenderMan™ DSO. This programme distributes the hair on the character, extracts information from the simulator and runs a "builder" which has information about every hair's colour, length, taper and unique characteristics.

*Shrek*, which had some fairly stiff-looking humans, every character in *Monsters, Inc.* was successfully depicted. Sulley is large, furry and surprisingly gentle; Boo is adorable, while Randall has just the right amount of sliminess.

*Monsters, Inc.*'s success was largely a result of the level of realistic human emotion portrayed by the characters. Good casting and voice direction played a part, but Pixar's animators and technical staff deserve most of the credit.

## Key Animators

The animation team hit a high point with the film, and demonstrated that Pixar's digital characters could show a range of emotion unequaled by other studios. A key change was the introduction of lead-character animators assigned for each of the main players – John Kahrs (Sulley), Andrew Gordon (Mike) and Dave Devan (Boo). This gave each character a more consistent personality, as each animator was responsible for "acting" the role. One scene of particular strength is when Sulley puts Boo to bed and slowly he realizes that he is growing quite fond of her. This emotional change was done purely through facial expression and body movement, and was the mark of a master animator.

## Technical Advances

As in all their films, Pixar strove to bring the technology behind *Monsters, Inc.* to the next level. The technical team developed a new application, "Geppetto", to add control points to a character, acting much like the strings on a puppet. This new software gave the animators unprecedented control over a character's motion, and meant that the lead characters – Sulley, Mike and Boo – were almost 40 percent more controllable than Al, the most complex of *Toy Story II*'s characters.

The biggest technical leap was in the realistic depiction of hair, fur and clothing. This advance greatly added to the realism of the film. Characters no longer looked plastic, and clothing was no longer limited to spandex. Pixar scientists created a software tool called Fizt (an amalgamation of the words "physics tool"), which simulated the millions of hairs on Sulley's fur, as well as the effects of forces, such as gravity and wind. This allowed the animation team to concentrate on getting the character's motion right, and the hair, fur and clothing were added later.

It was nominated for Best Animated Feature in 2002, but lost out to DreamWorks' *Shrek*.

# FINDING NEMO

Pixar's fourth feature, *Finding Nemo* (2003), is the studio's biggest success to date. The film set an all-time box office record for an animated feature, dethroning Disney's *Lion King*. *Nemo* is very different in tone from other Pixar films.

## Beginning of a Long Journey

Directed by Andrew Stanton, writer of all Pixar's previous films, it explores the relationship of a father and his lost son, Nemo – a clown fish – and is set on Australia's Great Barrier Reef. The film begins when Nemo is just an egg. Through a violent and traumatic event, Nemo (Alexander Gould) loses his mother and his siblings. Being the sole survivor puts tremendous pressure on Nemo's father, Marlin (Albert Brooks), to protect and care for his only son. The problem is that Marlin goes too far, and overprotects Nemo to the point of compulsion. Nemo, of course, wants to break out on his own, and in an act of rebellion, swims past the reef into open water, where he is captured by a scuba-diving dentist, who takes him back to his Sydney aquarium.

Marlin immediately dashes off in pursuit of Nemo, and embarks on a 1,000-mile journey down the Great Barrier Reef to Sydney. On the way, he meets a memory-challenged fish named Dory (Ellen DeGeneres) and encounters a group of reef sharks, dangerous jellyfish, surfer-dude turtles, a whale and a gregarious pelican. Finally, Marlin reaches Sydney and attempts a daring rescue of his son from the tropical fish tank.

## Leading the Way

The journey is more than just a physical one. Marlin undergoes a transformation, from being an awkward, inward-looking character to one who becomes much more confident. Dory also experiences a metamorphosis. The change in these characters was genuine, not a tacked-on artifact, the technique so prevalent in many children's films. The writing, direction and character development were of an extremely high standard, and set a precedent for animated features.

The ocean scenes were very lush and brilliantly colored. Pixar's lighting team managed to evoke perfectly the shimmering sunlight that occurs in the shallow tide pools of a tropical reef. This was not an easy task, as other underwater films such as *The Little Mermaid* can attest.

© Disney Enterprises Inc./Pixar Animation Inc.

### Dory and Marlin

As well as creating realistic water, Pixar's *Nemo* team had to understand the effects of water on the action and characters. The animators had to learn to read the surge and swell, and study how fast the water is flowing. The camera people needed to understand the effects of water on underwater photography, and it was vital for the lighting experts to learn how far one can see underwater.

### Jellyfish

Pixar's technical team looked into the elements needed to create photorealistic water – the floating particles, foggy matter and shafts of light – and designed all of the individual elements using the software that was on hand. They did tests using four ocean scenes, two above water and two underwater, to see if they could re-create real footage of the sea.

### Nemo

In order to learn how to animate swimming fish, a number of the crew spent a day at the Monterey Bay Aquarium. During production of the film, Pixar worked with an ichthyologist, who advised them on the particular movements and behavior of the types of fish they were animating.

*The Little Mermaid* » 277  *The Lion King* » 304

© Disney Enterprises Inc./Pixar Animation Inc.

## A Fishy Business

The fish in *Finding Nemo* presented a unique animation challenge. Most animated characters have bodies and hands with which to express themselves. Fish, however, are largely giant heads, with small fins for "hands". Pixar's animators had to rely on facial expressions and quick body motions to bring these characters to life. In addition to the fish, the human characters were a great advance on previous Pixar films. Animating the human form is the most difficult challenge an animator faces, and it was no different with this film. While *Nemo*'s audience would never have seen a talking fish, they would be highly critical if the animation of the humans was awkward or unrealistic, so the Pixar animators had to make sure they got it just right. It took Disney the better part of a decade before his studio mastered the art of human animation, and it seems to have taken Pixar a similar amount of time.

With *Finding Nemo*'s success, Pixar had four huge hits in a row and produced one of the best-selling animated films of all time. Pixar and the CGI film-making style it helped to invent are Hollywood's new animated royalty.

© Disney Enterprises Inc./Pixar Animation Inc.

# DREAMWORKS

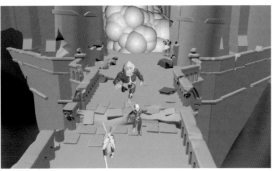

Shrek 2™ & © 2004 DreamWorks L.L.C.

The allying of DreamWorks and Pacific Data Images (PDI) resulted in another big force in the world of CGI features. PDI/DreamWorks has produced several very successful features to date, including *Antz* and the two *Shrek* films. Founded in 1980, PDI was one of the original computer animation companies. Throughout the 1980s and early 1990s, they survived where a number of early studios failed, and by 1996, were one of the top CGI production facilities. With the success of Pixar's *Toy Story*, Hollywood was looking to produce more CG animated features, and in March 1996, PDI signed a co-production deal with DreamWorks SKG to create original computer-generated feature-films. This turned PDI from a production facility into a fully fledged animation studio.

## Antz

PDI's first feature was *Antz* (1998), which debuted at the same time as Pixar's *A Bug's Life*. While both films explored the subject of ant colonies, Antz was much darker and more adult than *A Bug's Life*. The film stars Woody Allen and a host of other A-list stars (such as Gene Hackman and Sylvester Stallone) in an ant world that is downright Orwellian, with the ant hill representing the socialist worker state. Visually, *Antz* was spectacular, with design cues taken from films such as *Metropolis* and *Brazil*.

 *Antz* offered PDI a number of technical challenges. The vast number of ants in the colony required the animation of crowds to be done automatically. The software developed by PDI made it possible for the directors to include three times as many wide-angle shots of the ant-colony interior than were originally planned. A new suite of tools was developed to simulate the fluid dynamics of the huge flood near the end of the film, another advance pioneered by Pixar.

 They also developed a robust facial animation system for *Antz*. The system simulates the muscles and bones of the face, creating extremely lifelike results. Compared to Pixar's system at the time, PDI's facial animation system had a much higher degree of realism, giving the characters a much more subtle range of facial expressions.

 *Antz* was successful enough for the relationship between PDI and DreamWorks to continue. In February 2000, DreamWorks acquired the majority interest

Shrek 2™ & © 2004 DreamWorks LLC.

## Shrek 2

*Shrek 2*'s animators made use of the technological advances that had occurred since *Shrek* was released in 2001. By using a software program called a shader, Donkey's fur was made to react to environmental conditions, Fiona's skin and hair was given realistic texture and movement and the characters' eyes were given a lifelike sparkle.

## Shrek, Donkey and Fiona

The characters are set up based on an anatomically correct representation of bones, muscles and fat layers. They are then posed by animators who create their movement and performance before the final lighting is applied to the scene. Courtesy of DreamWorks Pictures.

## Puss in Boots

Representative of how CG characters are animated, a wireframe of Puss in Boots is pictured here. The colored icons represent joints, to which the animators apply rotations to pose the character. Low-resolution stand-in models are used to work out the character's final movements before the final pose is created with the high-resolution model. The final scene is then ready. Courtesy of DreamWorks Pictures.

in PDI to form PDI/DreamWorks. The next film released by the studio was *Shrek*, PDI's second animated feature film, in 2001.

## Shrek

*Shrek* turned the classic Disney fairy tale on its head. The story concerns Shrek (Mike Myers), an ogre who has been tossed out of his bog by the evil prince Farquaad (John Lithgow). In an attempt to win back his bog, Shrek offers to rescue the Princess Fiona (Cameron Diaz). Tagging along for comic relief is Donkey (Eddie Murphy).

*Shrek* was a big leap forward for PDI. While *Antz* was about a colony of rather similar-looking characters, *Shrek*'s characters were far more diverse and complex in their appearance. Shrek had an incredibly expressive face, probably more so than any prior CGI film. The realistic-looking hair and clothing of many of the characters in the film added to the richness of the visuals.

In terms of animation, the most successful characters were Donkey and Shrek. The humans looked rather stiff in comparison: getting the human form exactly right is still the ultimate goal for animators.

The visuals were beautiful and truly brought a storybook to life Settings included wide fields of grass waving in the wind, dark forests and medieval castles. The environments were also built not just as backdrops, but as real places, and characters left footprints in the grass as they walked. These were the subtle touches that made the world of *Shrek* so realistic.

The film was a huge box office success, and went on to win the first Oscar ever awarded for Best Animated Feature, beating Pixar's *Monsters, Inc.* for the title. With that award, PDI/DreamWorks set itself up as Pixar's main rival.

*Shrek 2* was released in 2004, and featuring some startling new developments in CG animation, set a new box-office record.

# BLUE SKY

New York-based Blue Sky was the third major CGI studio to release a feature film at the dawn of the new millennium. The studio had a long history in the computer-animation business, and this experience served them well when it came to making high-end CGI features.

## Commercial Success

The history of Blue Sky goes back to the dawn of computer graphics and the seminal CGI film *Tron*. Many of the founders of Blue Sky met at MAGI, one of the main studios responsible for the CGI in that ground-breaking film. MAGI was founded in 1987 and went on to make a mark in commercials, branching out into effects and character animation for features. By 1997, Blue Sky was one of the top studios on the East Coast, and they were purchased by Fox that year for the express purpose of developing and releasing feature-length animated films.

Their first film, *Ice Age*, was set in the snowy world of the early Ice Age. The story revolved around three characters: a woolly mammoth (Ray Romano); an irreverent, unsocialized giant sloth (John Leguizamo); and a scheming saber-toothed tiger (Dennis Leary). Together, this group of mismatched characters find a human baby and try to return him to his tribe.

## Light Fantastic

Directed by Chris Wedge, the film had a very soft and beautiful look. From the beginning, Blue Sky's renderer, dubbed CGI Studio, was its secret weapon. Originally developed by a doctor of physics and a NASA engineer, CGI Studio used such advanced techniques as ray tracing and global illumination to simulate physically the way light travels through a scene. This method was much more accurate than the rendering methods used by Pixar and PDI, producing incredibly realistic images.

This realism was evident in the representation of the snow and ice in the film. A glacier has a translucent quality that is very hard to match, but CGI Studio did an excellent job of duplicating the complex scattering of light through the icy scenes. Blue Sky had the most realistic renderer of all the CGI studios, and they used it to create a

### Sid the Sloth

Once the 3D version of Sid the Sloth was complete, the animators could get to work. An "X-ray" image of him was completed, allowing them to see his "muscles" and skin and understand how they are connected, and therefore how he moved. By manipulating the X-ray controls, they were able to arrange Sid into the required position.

© 20th Century Fox

### Diego

Blue Sky's film-makers spent time studying Ice Age artifacts, including woolly mammoth bones, and talking to paleontologists to ensure that their film had its basis in reality rather than in the realms of their imaginations.

Chris Wedge

Chris Wedge, the director of *Ice Age*, played a key role in developing Blue Sky's lighting software which was used to great effect in the film. Known as ray tracing, the software re-creates the effects of ambient light, and was employed to copy the way in which light bounces off objects and living creatures, creating realistic shade and shadows.

much more stylized look than in other features released at the same time. In places, *Ice Age* almost looks like a stop-motion feature rather than a CGI feature.

## Super Scrat

The characters in *Ice Age* were well designed, and fitted perfectly into the world created for them by the animators. The main characters' fur was not overly realistic, but worked well enough. Humans, as always, are a challenge for CG animators, but Blue Sky's humans were highly stylized; they animated beautifully and integrated well with the "cartoony" animal characters. The film's opening sequence was probably one of the most hilarious and thrilling of any animated feature. Scrat, a small squirrel in search of an acorn, manages to create an avalanche of epic proportions.

*Ice Age* was very successful and Fox ordered a second feature from them: *Robots* (2005).

# CONTEMPORARY TV ANIMATION

© Cartoon Network, Warner Bros. Animation

With the resounding success of CGI features and an increased viewership by adults, animation has grown into a booming industry. Two series in particular have emerged as clear pop stars – *The Powerpuff Girls* and *SpongeBob SquarePants*.

## Girl Power

*The Powerpuff Girls* originally started out as the Whoopass Girls in creator Craig McCracken's (b. 1971) student project *Whoopass Stew!*. McCracken began his career at Cartoon Network working on *2 Stupid Dogs* (1993–94) and Genndy Tartakovsky's (b. 1970) *Dexter's Laboratory* (1996 to date). After McCracken got the green light for a series, the title changed as well as the superpower-supplying secret ingredient from a can of Whoopass to Chemical X.

McCracken said: "The biggest influence on *Powerpuff Girls* was the 1960s (live-action) *Batman* show. As a kid I watched it in all seriousness and I would get really frustrated that my parents would be laughing at it. It wasn't until I was older and I rediscovered the show did I realize that it was a total joke. So when I set out to make

### Powerpuff Girls

Half cartoon, half anime, *The Powerpuff Girls* began life as the Whoopass Girls, who were created by Professor Utonium by combining sugar, spice and all things nice with a can of Whoopass. They also featured in a film with the Amoeba Boys called *A Sticky Situation*.

### Powerpuff Girls with Mojo Jojo

Creator Craig MacCracken was involved in all stages of *The Powerpuff Girls Movie*. Whereas the TV series was storyboarded in the US and then animated in Korea, the team were able to work on each shot of the film to ensure it was as they wanted. They were able to use digital-animation techniques that gave them a greater range of motion and more control over the shots.

Prime-TIme in the 1990s » 314

© Cartoon Network, Warner Bros. Animation

## SpongeBob SquarePants

SpongeBob, who became something of an unlikely cult icon, lives in Bikini Bottom. The cartoon appealed as much to adults as it did to children, and was a breath of fresh air among the tongue-in-cheek innuendos paramount in so many other cartoons.

© NickToon Productions

*Powerpuff Girls* I wanted to create a show that could work on two different levels... kids would like the fun and action aspect and adults would get the jokes and the campy aspect."

## Cult TV

With the aid of supervising producer Tartakovsky, *The Powerpuff Girls* series debuted in 1998 and quickly developed a cult following across varying demographics, most surprisingly young boys. Up until that time, children's programing executives believed boys would not watch shows with female lead characters. Other networks were soon scrambling to find their "girl power" series. The success of the TV show spurred Cartoon Network's parent company, Warner Bros., to venture into the first animated theatrical feature bearing the Cartoon Network name. Going back and telling the origin story of Blossom, Bubbles and Buttercup, *The Powerpuff Girls Movie* arrived in theaters in 2002. However, the height of the craze had died down and the film, though profitable, received a disappointing box-office gross. Despite the lackluster performance of the feature, *The Powerpuff Girls* remains a pop cultural milestone, teaching the world that girls can kick butt too.

## Underwater Success

*SpongeBob SquarePants* burst on to the scene in 1999 and instantly returned a zany, whimsical tone to the TV cartoon world. Originally a marine biology teacher, creator Stephen Hillenburg went back to school to get a degree in experimental animation from CalArts. He broke into animation as a storyboard artist on Nickelodeon's *Rocko's Modern Life*, later serving as a creative producer, writer and director on the series. Bringing his love of drawing and sea life together, he created SpongeBob, the eternal optimist, who quickly became a star. With its mix of gag humor and intelligent, mature writing, the series attracted a wide range of viewers. Comedian/voice actor Tom Kenny, who had worked on *Rocko's Modern Life*, created SpongeBob's distinct voice. After 60 episodes, Hillenburg decided to take a hiatus from the series to work on a planned feature based on the show. The character has become a bona fide star, and the show ranks, along with Nickelodeon's *Rugrats*, as one of the most successful animated cable-television series.

For the next generation, *The Powerpuff Girls* and *SpongeBob SquarePants* have set the standard for what contemporary TV animation can be and whom it can reach.

# SMALL-SCREEN STARS

In addition to *The Powerpuff Girls* and *SpongeBob SquarePants*, other cartoons began to emerge as animated stars.

### Adult Swim Block

Riding the cult success of *Space Ghost Coast to Coast*, Cartoon Network, in 2001, launched its Adult Swim programing block. Series like *The Brak Show*, *Harvey Birdman, Attorney-At-Law* and *Sealab 2021* used new technology to create postmodern spoofs of many of the 1960s and 1970s Hanna-Barbera characters. The lineup's *Aqua Teen Hunger Force* quickly became a cult hit with its irreverent fast-food heroes and adult themes. Adult Swim also brings mature anime to the US like *Cowboy Bebop* and *Detective Conan*, and resurrects canceled prime-time cartoons like *Home Movies* and *Mission Hill*.

### Anime Action

Outside of the Adult Swim block, the network saw other success. In 2001, Cartoon Network debuted *Samurai Jack*, created by Tartakovsky. Influenced by the UPA style and Japanese print art, the series attracts both young and adult viewers. Tartakovsky said, "The goal for *Samurai Jack* was to create an action series that focused on visual storytelling rather than on dialogue, so there would be room for great action and character drama."

When it came to action, anime led the way. But not since *Pokémon* had a series seen such success as the *DragonBall* franchise. The series gathered a devoted following, who tuned in to the epic battles that could stretch out for several episodes.

In addition, Bruce Timm, one of the creative forces behind *The New Adventures of Batman/Superman*, shaped the new Justice League, teaming some of DC Comics' legendary superheroes. The Kids' WB! aired DC Comics' *Teen Titans*, Japanese sensation *Yu-Gi-Oh!*, wrestling-inspired *¡Mucha Lucha!* and the new incarnation of *Astro Boy*. Warner Bros. and Cartoon Network brought back *Looney Tunes* icons Daffy Duck, Porky Pig and Marvin the Martian in their own series, *Duck Dodgers*.

### Nick's successes

SpongeBob was not the only pop celebrity to emerge from Nickelodeon. Starting in short interstitials, John A. Davis and Steve Oedekerk created boy genius Jimmy Neutron and his robot dog Goddard. The Oscar-nominated CG feature *Jimmy Neutron: Boy Genius* preceded the TV series, which debuted in 2002. This allowed the series to utilize the CG elements created for the feature, giving it an unprecedented quality for a CGI TV series.

© DNA Productions / Nickelodeon Movies / O Entertainment

**Jimmy Neutron**

John A. Davis of DNA Productions first created a boy genius in the form of Johnny Quasar, using LightWave 3D software. They had some success with the short, and after being joined by Steve Oedekerk, the character was refined into the more childlike Jimmy Neutron. Using LightWave and Messiah, the CG-animated feature was the first of its kind to be completely produced with out-of-the-box software.

© Klasky-Csupo Productions

**Rugrats – Phil and Chuckie**

The idea for the *Rugrats* originally came from Arlene Klasky; to create a cartoon from the perspective of a one-year-old. The original character, Tommy Pickles, was based on Arlene's son. Klasky collaborated with Gabor Csupo and Paul Germain in creating the final series which premiered on Nickelodeon in 1991.

**Samurai Jack**

The visual style of *Samurai Jack* is impressive in its use of well-known elements from anime and film. Split screens, silhouetted panoramic views, intense close-ups and three repetitions of the same attack are all used to great effect.

© Cartoon Network Studios, Rough Draft Studios

Creator Butch Hartman, a former writer/director on *Johnny Bravo*, brought to the network *The Fairly OddParents*, following the mishaps of Timmy Turner and his inept fairy godparents, Cosmo and Wanda. The success of the series spurred the network to produce the television movie *The Fairly OddParents: Abra-Catastrophe*, and put forth plans for a theatrical feature.

Created by Arlene Klasky, *Rocket Power* emerged as a solid hit with its group of extreme sports-loving kids. In 2001, Nickelodeon launched *Invader ZIM* from indie comic book artist Jhonen Vasquez. Following the misadventures of a tiny alien that tries hopelessly to conquer Earth, the smart series never found a foothold in the network's more child-oriented lineup and was canceled in 2003, despite a cult fan base.

With the continued success of *Rugrats*, Nickelodeon and animation company Klasky Csupo created the special "All Growed Up", which featured the Rugrats as middle-school students. Tweens and teens who grew up with the series enjoyed watching Tommy, Chucky and Angelica dealing with teen issues, and Nickelodeon launched the spin-off series *All Grown Up* in 2003. That same year also saw the premiere of *My Life as a Teenage Robot*, which started out as a segment on the anthology series *Oh Yeah! Cartoons*.

## Disney's New Generation

Disney's first new star came in 2000. Created by illustrator Gary Baseman and *Cheers* producers Bill and Cherie Steinkellner, the stylized *Teacher's Pet* became a hit, led by the voice work of stage and film star Nathan Lane. In 2004, the characters made the jump to the big screen.

*Kim Possible* debuted in 2001 and brought "girl power" to Disney. Following the adventures of teenage secret-agent Kim Possible and her bumbling friend Ron Stoppable, the series works equally well as a superhero-show spoof and as a bona fide action adventure.

In addition, the theatrical success of *Lilo & Stitch* spawned a TV series, following Lilo and Stitch's attempts to round up various experimental creatures. Another notable series for Disney is *The Proud Family*, created by *Bebe's Kids* director Bruce W. Smith, which follows African American Penny Proud and her crazy family.

# THE MATRIX

*The Matrix* trilogy brought special effects and digital character techniques to a whole new level. Directed by the Wachowski brothers, *The Matrix* (1999), *The Matrix Reloaded* (2003) and *The Matrix Revolutions* (2003) were incredibly successful and had a huge influence on the CGI community.

## Real World or Cyber World?

Like *Tron*, the very first CGI feature, *The Matrix* centered around the world of cyberspace. Unlike *Tron*, in which the line between real and virtual was very distinct, *The Matrix* presented cyberspace exactly as the real world, but with the addition of some very dazzling special effects.

*The Matrix*'s version of cyberspace provided a measure of how far CGI had come in just a few decades. The world could be pristine and synthetic, as in *Tron*, but could also be a gritty CG-generated reality. The film introduced several striking effects, including the much-since-copied "bullet time" effect, which created wildly fast camera movements around ultra-slow-motion events. The film used CGI to create realistic virtual sets, while the directors had total freedom in camera movement, using a new technique called virtual cinematography.

## Digital Cast

In addition to mind-blowing special effects, the films also employed a lot of character animation. The real feat in *The Matrix* trilogy was not the creation of new and fantastic characters, but the creation of digital replacements for the live-action cast. These were used in countless scenes, and the switch between real and virtual actors was flawless.

One of the most notable scenes in the trilogy was in *The Matrix Reloaded*, where the hero Neo (Keanu Reaves) battles several hundred Agent Smiths. There were several points in this sequence where the film cut seamlessly between a live-action Keanu Reeves and his digital counterpart. The ability to cut between digital and live-action versions of the same character so effortlessly provided the Wachowski brothers

### The Matrix Reloaded

John Gaeta, who was visual-effects supervisor of *The Matrix* trilogy, was the innovator of the "bullet-time" photography. This was achieved by using high-speed cameras, which in some cases approached 12,000 35 mm frames per second. When slowed down to the standard 24 frames per second of standard film, actions appear to be very fluid and slow-moving.

### APUs ready for battle

The APUs featured in *The Matrix Revolutions*, and were created from concept artwork that was made into a computer model. The computer models were used to visualize script scenarios, and to produce renderings to assist in manufacture and assembly of the APU components.

*Tron* » 268  Digital Domain » 306

& © 2004 Go Fish Pictures

**Millennium Actress – head-shot**

This is a hand-drawn film about legendary Japanese actress Chiyoko Fujiwara, who is persuaded to tell her story to a documentary maker and his cameraman. They become literal witnesses to her extraordinary story as she recounts her career, moving from space to feudal Japan in the process.

& © 2004 Go Fish Pictures

*Cat in Space* (2002), written/directed/scored by the rock-music duo "Tree of Life" a.k.a. "Kuno and Kazuka", was an imaginative space adventure featuring a funny animal cat that looked like a sluttish, foul-mouthed Goth parody of *Hello Kitty*, in the tradition of such American animation as *The Ren & Stimpy Show* and *Beavis & Butt-head*. It was popular enough to spin off a late-night TV series, *Tamala's Wild Party* (2004).

## Japanese TV

New hit-TV animated series included the juvenile *Hamtaro Tales* (2000) about a young girl's happy pet hamster and his happy friends; *Inu Yasha* (2000), a fantasy-drama featuring supernatural monsters typical of medieval Japanese folklore (another adaptation of a popular manga by Rumiko Takahashi); and *Love Hina* (2000), a teen romantic comedy revolving around a shy, easily embarrassed boy forced to become the manager/caretaker of an all-girl student dorm. The allure of *DragonBall*-style art and light fantasy-adventure continued in *One Piece* (1999), a pirate-world burlesque epic by Eiichiro Oda (b. 1975), an acknowledged fan of DB's Akira Toriyama. *Beyblade* (2001) was the next *Pokémon*-like hit series based upon a heavily merchandised game or toy. An elaborate fantasy world in which boys everywhere compete for prestige in national and global Beyblade tournaments, it had its popularity reinforced by actual tournaments organized by the manufacturers of Beyblade spinning tops (including electronic and remote-controlled tops, and accessories). At the opposite extreme, *Hikaru no Go* (2001), based upon the manga by Yumi Hotta and Takeshi Obata, made news by unexpectedly revitalizing interest among the youth in the ancient Japanese chess-like game of Go. Hikaru, an undisciplined schoolboy, solves his modern social problems after learning to think and develop strategy after he is possessed by the friendly spirit of a ninth-century Go master.

In the early part of the new century, there was a vogue for short (usually 12 or 13 episodes) futuristic sci-fi TV series in interstellar settings with visually spectacular CGI astronomical panoramas and complex shiny machines, often ending on a cliff-hanger; those that were popular were followed up with a "part 2" conclusion a year later. *Crest of the Stars* (1999), *Pilot Candidate* (2000), *Vandread* (2001) and *GeneShaft* (2001) were among the most outstanding of these. Broccoli, a new design company, took the "cute fantasy little girl" stereotype and emphasized it to the point of self-parody in such popular comedy-fantasy series as *Di Gi Charat* (1999) and *Galaxy Angel* (2001), both produced by the Madhouse studio, and *Sugar: A Little Snow Fairy* (2001), produced by J.C. Staff.

### The Hit-Makers

Two TV series based upon their studios' hit theatrical features of the previous decade were Production I.G's *Ghost in the Shell: Stand Alone Complex* (2002) and Madhouse's *Ninja Scroll: The Series* (2003), while a new TV adaptation of *Astro Boy* was created by Tezuka Production Co. for his "birthday". He was said, in his 1953 manga origin story, to have been created in 2003 and his character was updated with state-of-the-art animation.

Two TV series achieved critical and popular success for quality and originality even though they were clearly inspired by foreign hit movies or TV series: *Noir* (2001), about young women professional killers, similar to *La Femme Nikita*; and *Witch Hunter Robin* (2002), about an agency assigned to hunt "witches" (people with psychic abilities such as teleportation and telepathy) who use their powers in criminal ways – a cross between a police-procedural series and *The X-Files*.

### Something Different

TV series that stood out as imaginatively different included *Boogiepop Phantom* (2000), a psychological horror fantasy. *NieA_7* (2001) and *Haibane-Renmei* (2002) are both dreamlike fantasies, written and designed by Yoshitoshi Abe, that question the nature of reality. *Arjuna* (2001), directed by Shoji Kawamori, is a didactically pro-ecological fantasy. *Hellsing* (2001) pushed graphic horror on TV in new directions and to new limits. *.hack//SIGN* (2002) created a visually striking virtual fantasy gaming world in which role-playing fans could become trapped. *Last Exile* (2003) is a stunning creation of a socially grim nineteenth-

**Noir**

Tsukimura Ryoei's stylish TV series had opening credits featuring *James Bond*-inspired animation and a great soundtrack. Featuring two female assassins, *Noir* has plentiful shoot-outs that resemble the sword fights of samurai dramas, but no blood is spilled.

**Noir – Mireille**

Mireille is one of the two assassins that make up the "Noir" partnership. This model sheet shows some of the early sketches of this most stylish of assassins.

Mireille
collection of poses

© Nekojiru – Yamato Do Co. Ltd./ Nekojiru Family

century-style world with Vernean flying machines. *Wolf's Rain* (2003) is an impressive, though gloomy, tale of a hidden clan of werewolves trying to survive in a decaying over-urbanized future world. *Planetes* (2003) is a technologically accurate, hard-science sci-fi comedy about astronaut "garbage collectors" assigned to clean up debris in near-Earth orbits, and *Paranoia Agents* (2004), Satoshi Kon's first TV series, is a psychological thriller.

## Art-House Influence

Two art films that got high-profile OAV releases were *Cat Soup* (2001), by director Tatsuo Sato (b. 1964), a tribute to an early 1990s surrealistic underground comic by "Nekojiru" (which was popular with animators and was produced shortly after the disturbed artist's suicide), and *Voices of a Distant Star*, by Makoto Shinkai (b. 1973), a 25-minute sci-fi romance that looked like a professional production, but was written and produced entirely by the prize-winning creator on home equipment.

### Cat Soup

Director Tatsuo Sato explained that he and his staff constructed *Cat Soup* – an unconventional work – by creating a series of distinct images and then simply stitching them together. This visually stunning, free-form short used only the loose guidelines of the original manga to govern the narrative flow.

© Nekojiru – Yamato Do Co. Ltd./ Nekojiru Family

# THE NEW AND THE TRADITIONAL

There were some notable titles among the more traditional commercial OAV productions. *FLCL* (pronounced "fooly cooly"), a 2000–01 surrealistic teen-comedy miniseries by director Kazuya Tsurumaki (b. 1966), careered wildly from no animation (a fast-forward viewing of manga panels) through traditional animation enhanced with computer graphics, possibly signifying the emotional confusion of adolescence.

## James Bond Tradition

*R.O.D. (Read or Die)*, a 2001 three-episode miniseries directed by Kouji Masunari, both spoofed and was a great secret-agent drama in the *James Bond* movie tradition; secret agents of the British Library save the world from destruction by megalomaniacal master criminals. It was even more popular with three episodes edited together into an OAV feature, and it spun off a *R.O.D.* TV series sequel.

### Mt Head

Since Winsor McCay's very first animated films, animators have reveled in their ability to transform the visual world. In *Mt Head*, Yamamura exercises this fundamental capability to an extraordinary degree, creating worlds in constant flux, characterized by dazzling visual images that shift and change in the blink of an eye.

### Elmo Aardvark – Earth

The *Elmo Aardvark* series received a special Annie Award from the International Animated Film Society (ASIFA-Hollywood) and the Monsieur Pluc Award at Annecy due its inventiveness. LokoMotion and Bisonic Aural Gratification Systems were developed especially for the series.

© Will Ryan & Co. Ltd

### Elmo Aardvark & VaVa LaVoom

Pictured here are Elmo Aardvark and VaVa LaVoom. A feature film based on the outer-space adventures of Elmo has been on several development slates in the intervening years.

### Atom Films & Bill Plympton

*25 Ways to Quit Smoking*, *How To Kiss*, *Parking* and *The Wiseman* are just four of Bill Plympton's films featured on AtomFilms.com. These and seven other Plympton films can be viewed online.

## A Flash of Inspiration

AtomFilms.com, IFILM.com and Macromedia's Shockwave.com created the most excitement among independent film-makers by establishing a new marketplace for animated short films. For instance, IFILM had great success putting Spike and Mike's Festival of Animation online, while Shockwave linked up with comic-book and animation-legend Stan Lee to screen his popular *7th Portal* series. Aardman made the live-action/animated *Angry Kid* for AtomFilms, which also provided a venue for the films of Bill Plympton. It also signed Tim Burton, who produced the *Stainboy* series, as well as *South Park* creators Trey Parker and Matt Stone; however, the latter's first film was shelved after it proved too gross for AtomFilms' viewers.

Among broadcasters who got involved, the most interesting was the nascent Oxygen network, which simulcast its offbeat *X-Chromosome* anthology series online, including *Fat Girl* by Prudence Fenton, Allee Willis and April Winchell.

## End of a Good Thing?

The lack of viable business models that caused the dot-bust eventually hit Web animation by the end of 2000. Many companies closed, and those that survived endured massive layoffs, with Shockwave taking over AtomFilms. A few major players survived, including Mondo Media, which was able to develop a viable syndication model for such series as *The God and Devil Show* (2000), and using DVD sales and merchandising to increase revenues from series like *Happy Tree Friends* (2002). For its part, AtomFilms has used a subscription model for such in-demand series as Aardman's *Wallace and Gromit's Cracking Contraptions*.

The use of Web technologies, especially Flash, has also found markets beyond the Internet itself. Thus, in 2001, Nelvana's prime-time show *Quads* became the first TV series produced using Flash, which also made it easier to show it on the Web.

In the late 1980s independent producers were looking for ways of financing their productions and started looking to the world market. And production companies like Hanna-Barbera were looking for new animation for their broadcasters. Mike Young, at Siriol Animation in Wales, could not sell a show directly to US broadcasters, so he partnered with Hanna-Barbera and Booker Entertainment to produce television series *Super Ted* (1985) and *Fantastic Max* (1988). Young also co-produced *Once Upon A Forest* (1993), a movie for FOX with Hanna-Barbera and HTV.

## Plenty of Opportunities

There were advantages for animation producers to work in Europe or Canada. France had established in 1946 the government agency Centre National de la Cinematographie (CNC), which has helped to subsidize French productions. Canada established a tax incentive for production companies that shot films in the country. By partnering with French or Canadian production companies, US and other producers were able to reap the financial benefits.

In the United States, in the late 1980s, producers like Ted Kopplar, of World Events Productions, saw the financial benefits of co-production with a French company. World Events was already partnered with Calico Entertainment in 1988 on *Denver the Last Dinosaur*. During the second season World Events took on the French partner IDDH. Koplar exchanged production services and funding from the French company for international rights and toy deals.

Calico Entertainment later partnered with Zodiac Entertainment on *Widget* (1990–91). Calico also partnered with Zodiac and Alligator Films, a Belgium production company, for *Mr Bogus* (1991–93). In 1992 Zodiac and Calico partnered again on *Twinkle*, a series based on the popular Olympic mascot from the 1992 Korean Games. This co-production was led by the Korean broadcaster MBC, along with Sei Young Studios, a Korean production service that had worked on all of Calico's previous productions.

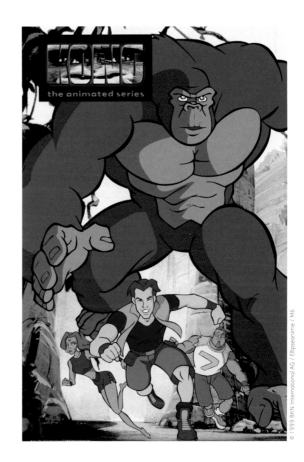

**Kong, The Animated Series**

The story leading up to the series explains that a new Kong is born from DNA taken by Lorna Jenkins, from the original Kong and a small amount of human DNA taken from her grandson, Jason Jenkins. Kong and his prehistoric island are once again under threat, this time from gigantic prehistoric creatures and monstrous DNA mutants.

Japanese and American Co-Production » 372

## Kong, The Animated Series

Jason Jenkins and his friend Tan bring their teacher Ramon De La Porta to the island to show him the beauty of it, and of course Kong. Unfortunately De La Porta has other plans and steals the island's Primal Stones which control its balance. In each episode Jason, Tan, a shaman girl named Lua and Kong travel around the world to find the stones, restore balance to the island and thwart De La Porta once and for all.

## Multitude of Takeovers

In 1990, the broadcast networks' audiences dropped dramatically due to the advent of cable and the introduction of FOX-TV. The FCC relaxed Fin-Syn in 1991 and finally abolished it in 1995. This change opened up the opportunity for the major production companies like the Walt Disney Company to purchase the ABC network and for Warner Bros. to start WB TV network. These companies could now own what they aired.

The year 1995 was the turning point for many companies. Hanna-Barbera was purchased for its library of shows by the Turner Company (later to be a part of Warner Bros.), and the smaller studios like Fred Wolf Production, Ruby-Spears, Zodiac Entertainment, Calico Entertainment and many others started closing their doors for a lack of venues to sell their programs.

In 1990 Mike Young crossed over to the US to start Mike Young Productions. Using his connections in Europe he immediately produced the television series *Secret Garden* (1993–94) with S4C for ABC TV. He then produced Prince Charles' *Legend of Lochnagar* (1993) with ABC, Virgin and S4C.

## International Co-Production

In the early part of the twenty-first century, international co-production has become a necessity. The television series *Kong: The Animated Series* (2000) was conceived in the US by Stephanie Graizano of BKN, and produced with Ellipse Anime (France) and pasi (Philippine Animation Studio, Inc.). Both Ellipse Anime and pasi worked with their own outside services, including services in Korea, the Philippines and India. Co-productions like this can offer many benefits to the contributing partners, including production services at cost in exchange for regional distribution revenues, revenues for all from the adjusted gross and tax points and credits where applicable. Working with so many partners can have its drawbacks in communications, cultural differences and time zones.

An example of a truly international co-production model is the animated series *Max and the Mechanicals* (2004) for PBS (US). This is a co-production between Mike Young Productions (US), Sony Television Animation (US), PBS (US), Telegael (Ireland) and jadooWorks Animation Studio (India). Deals like this allow for partners to put in either cash, cash and services, or services as their participation.

As we get further into the twenty-first century co-production will be borderless. IDT Entertainment, Inc. has established a proprietary system, the Global Animation Protocol, for working together with other production companies worldwide. IDT Entertainment is bringing the financial resources of its parent company, IDT Corp., an international telecommunications company, to assist in deficit financing of co-productions, along with providing their own production resources to creative partner companies for television and features.

# REFERENCES

## BIBLIOGRAPHY

Adamson, J., *Tex Avery, King of Cartoons*, DeCapo Press, 1985

Barrier, M., *Hollywood Cartoons*, Oxford University Press, 1999

Beck, J., *The 50 Greatest Cartoons*, Turner Publishing, 1994

Beck, J., and Friedwald, W., *Looney Tunes and Merrie Melodies: A Complete Illustrated Guide to the Warner Bros. Cartoons*, Henry Holt, 1989

Beckerman, H., *Animation: The Whole Story*, Allworth & School of Visual Arts, 2003

Bendazzi, G., *Cartoons: One Hundred Years of Cinema Animation*, Indiana University Press, 1994

Cabarga, L., *The Fleischer Story*, DeCapo Press, 1995

Canemaker, J., *Walt Disney's Nine Old Men*, Disney Editions, 2001

Canemaker, J., *Winsor McCay: His Life and Art*, Abbeville Press, 1987

Clements, J., and McCarthy, H., *The Anime Encyclopedia: A Guide to Japanese Animation Since 1917*, Stone Bridge Press, 2001

Crafton, D., *Before Mickey*, MIT Press, 1982

Culhane, S., *Talking Animals and Other People: The Autobiography of One of Animation's Legendary Figures*, St Martin's Press, 1994

Erickson, H., *Television Cartoon Shows: An Illustrated Encyclopedia, 1949–1993*, McFarland, 1995

Ledoux, T. (ed.), *Anime Interviews: The First Five Years of Animerica, Anime & Manga Monthly*, Cadence Books, 1997

Ledoux, T., and Ranney, D., *The Complete Anime Guide: Japanese Animation Film Directory & Resource Guide*, Tiger Mountain Press, 1997

Lent, J. (ed.), *Animation in Asia and the Pacific*, Indiana University Press, 2001

Levi, A., *Samurai From Outer Space: Understanding Japanese Animation*, Open Court Publishing Co., 1996

Maltin, L., *The Disney Films*, Disney Editions, 2000

Maltin, L., *Of Mice and Magic: A History of American Animated Cartoons*, Plume Books, New American Library, 1980

Mangels, A., *Animation on DVD: The Ultimate Guide*, Stone Bridge Press, 2003

McCarthy, H., *Hayao Miyazaki: Master of Japanese Animation*, Stone Bridge Press, 1999

Merritt, R., and Kaufman, J. B., *Walt in Wonderland*, Indiana University Press, 1992

Patten, F., *Watching Anime, Reading Manga: 25 Years of Essays and Reviews*, Stone Bridge Press, 2004

Pilling, J. (ed.), *A Reader in Animation Studies*, John Libbey, 1997

Robinson, C., *Between Genius and Utter Illiteracy: A Story of Estonian Animation*, Varrak Publishing, 2003

Schneider, S., *That's All Folks! The Art of Warner Bros. Animation*, Henry Holt, 1990

Scott, K., *The Moose That Roared*, St Martin's Press, 2000

Smith, D., *Disney A to Z*, Hyperion, 1998

Stephenson, R., *The Animated Film*, The Tantivy Press, 1981

Webb, G., *The Animated Film Encyclopedia, 1900–1979*, McFarland, 2000

## MAGAZINES

*Animation Magazine*

*Animation Blast*

"Beyond Good and Evil: Piotr Dumala's Crime and Punishment", Issue 5.10, *Animation World Magazine*, January 2001

Janeva, M., "Bulgarian Animation: A Short Review", *Animation World Magazine*, June 2003

Knott, T. and Taylor F., "Bold and Beautiful: The Genius of Bulgarian Animation", pp. 72–73, *Ottawa 88 International Animation Festival Official Programme Book* Canadian Film Institute, 1988

Matuszewski, W., "Animated Film in Poland", pp. 8–18, *Holland Animation Film Festival Catalogue*, Holland Animation Film Festival, 1996

Pavlov, B., "Sixty Years Soyuzmultfilm", pp. 48–52, *Holland Animation Film Festival Catalogue*, Holland Animation Film Festival, 1996

## ORIGINAL JAPANESE & CHINESE FILM TITLES

**I: The Origin of the Art: pages 30–31**

*Imokawa Mukuzo Genkanban no Maki* • *Mukuzo Imokawa, the Concierge*

*Sarukani Gassen* • *The Battle of the Monkey and the Crab*

*Hanahekonai Meitou no Maki* • *Hanahekonai's New Sword, a.k.a. The Fine Sword*

*Taro no Banpei: Senkotei* • *Taro the Sentry; Submarine*

*Kitatu to Mizugepontpu* • *Atmospheric Pressure and the Suction Pump*

*Ninki no Shouten ni Tateru Goto Shinpei* • *The Spotlight is on Shinpei Goto*

*Usagi to Kame* • *The Tortoise and the Hare*

*Ubasute-yama* • *The Mountain Where Old Women Are Left to Die*

*Shiohara Tasuke* • *Tasuke Shiohara*

*Nonkina Tosan Ryugu Mairi* • *A Carefree Old Guy Visits the Ryugu*

*Suzumi Bune* • *Cooling Off on the Boat*

*Nihonichi no Momotaro* • *Momotaro is Japan's No. 1*

*Tako na Hone* • *Octopus Bones*

*Bunbuku Chagama* • *The Tale of the Lucky Teakettle*

*Kaeru wa Kaeru* • *A Frog is a Frog*

*Dobutsu Olympiku Taikai* • *The Animals' Olympics*

*Oira no Yakyuu* • *My Baseball*

*Komori* • *The Bat*

*Son Goku Monogatari* • *The Legend of Son Goku*

*Kujira* • *The Whale*

*Kuro Nyago* • *Black Kitty*

**II: Finding Its Voice: pages 52–53**

*Nansensu Monogatari: dai 1 hen, Sarugashima* • *A Shipwreck Tale: Part 1, Monkey Island*

*Nansensu Monogatari: dai 2 hen, Koizoku-bune* • *A Shipwreck Tale: Part 2, The Pirate Ship* [Note: *Nansensu Monogatari* is a pun that means both "A Shipwreck Tale" and "A Nonsense Tale"]

*Chikara to Onna no Yokonaka* • *The World of Power and Women*

*Tahchan no Kaitei Ryokou* • *Tahchan's Trip to the Bottom of the Sea*

*Osaru no Taigyo* • *The Monkey's Big Catch*

*Sora no Momotaro* • *Aerial Momotaro*

*Norakuro* • *Black Dog*

*Norakuro Nitohei — Kyoren no Maki* • *Buck Private Norakuro — Training*

*Norakuro Nitohei — Enshu no Maki* • *Buck Private Norakuro — Drills*

*Norakuro Gocho* • *Sergeant Norakuro*

*Norakuro Shoi — Nichiyabi no Kaijiken* • *2nd Lieutenant Norakuro — The Sunday Mystery*

*Koari no Itazura* • *The Mischievous Little Ant*

*Osaru Sankichi — Bakusen no Maki* • *Sankichi the Monkey — Air Defense Military Exercise*

*Kuroneko Banzai* • *Black Cat Hooray!*

**III: Technicolor Fantasies: pages 76–77**

*Genroku Koi Moyou: Sankichi to Osayo* • *Love in the Genroku Era: Sankichi and Osayo*

*Izakaya no Ichiya* • *A Night at a Tavern*

*Issun Bashi Chibisuke Monogatari* • *The Tale of Tiny Issun Bochi's Rescue*

*Benkei tai Ushiwaka* • *Benkei versus Ushiwaka*

*Kachikachiyama* • *The Hare's Revenge on the Tanuki*

*Musume Dojoji* • *The Girl at Dojo's Temple*

*Oira no Hijayi* • *My Emergency*

*Maabo no Shanin Kokuhei* • *Maabo, the Boy Pilot*

*Sora no Shanhai Sensen* • *Skies Over the Shanghai Battlegrounds*

*Sora no Arawashi* • *Aerial Ace*

**IV: The World War Two Era: pages 112–115**

*Ma-bo no Rakkasan Butai* • *Ma-bo's Paratroop Unit*

*Fuku-chan no Sensuikan* • *Fuku-chan and the Submarine*

*Spy Gekimetsu* • *Spies Defeated*

*Nippon Banzai* • *Hooray for Japan!*

*Osaru Sankichi — Boukan no Kaiheidan* • *Sankichi the Monkey's Marine Corps Air Defense*

*Osaru Sankichi — Tatakau Sensuikan* • *Sankichi the Monkey's Fighting Submarine*

*Ocho-fujin no Genso* • *Fantasy of the Butterfly Wife*

*Kaguya Hime* • *Princess Kaguya*

*Momotaro no Umiwashi* • *Momotaro's Sea Eagles*

*Kumo to Tulip* • *The Spider and the Tulip*

*Ari-chan* • *Ant Boy*

*Momotaro — Umi no Washi* • *Momotaro's Divinely-Blessed Sea Warriors*

*Gen-ei Toshi* • *Fantasy City*

*Ai* • *Love*

*Honoo no Fantasy* • *A Fantasy of Flames*

*Shin Takarajima* • *New Treasure Island*

*Ginga Shonentai* • *Boys' Space Patrol*

*Tenrankai no E* • *Pictures at an Exhibition*

*Sen-ya Ichi-ya Monogatari* • *The Thousand and One Nights*

*Cleopatra* • *Cleopatra, a.k.a. Cleopatra, Queen of Sex*

*Kanashimi no Belladonna* • *The Tragedy of Belladonna*

*Hinotori 2772: Ai no Cosmozone* • *Phoenix 2772, a.k.a. Space Firebird*

*Onboro Filumu* • *Broken-Down Film*

*Mori no densetsu* • *Legend of the Forest*

*Sun Wu Kong — Da Nao Tian Gong (Mandarin)/Da Nao Tien Gu (Cantonese)* •

**V: The Post-War Era: pages 142–143**

*Maho no Pen* • *The Magic Crayon*

*Suteneko Tora-chan* • *Tora-chan, the Abandoned Kitten*

*Tora-chan no Hanayome* • *Tora-chan and the Bride*

*Ousama no Shippo* • *The King's Tail*

*Dobutsu Daiyakyu Sen* • *The Animals' Great Baseball War*

*Yuki no Yoru no Yume* • *A Snowy Night's Dream*

**VI: Cartoons Mature: pages 174–175**

*Mori no Ongakukai* • *The Forest Concert*

*Kobito to Aomushi* • *The Gnome and the Green Caterpillar*

*Ari to Hato* • *The Ant and the Pigeon*

*Ko Usagi Monogatari* • *Story of the Little Rabbit*

*Kawataro Kappa* • *Kawataro the Kappa*

*Ukari Violin* • *The Happy Violin*

*Onbu Obake* • *Onbu, the Little Goblin*

*Taisei Shakuson* • *The Great Buddha*

*Kujira* • *The Whale*

*Yuri-sen* • *The Ghost Ship*

*Aru Machikado no Monogatari* • *Stories on a Street Corner*

*Ma Liang* • *The Magic Paintbrush*

**VII: To The Tube: pages 196–197**

*Koneko no Rakugaki* • *Doodling Kitty*

*Koneko no Studio* • *Kitty's Studio*

*Hakuja Den (Legend of the White Snake Enchantress)* • *Panda and the Magic Serpent*

*Shonen Sarutobi Sasuke (Sasuke, the Ninja Boy)* • *Magic Boy*

*Saiyuki (History of the Journey to the West)* • *Alakazam the Great*

*Hyotan Suzume* • *The Sparrow in the Empty Gourd*

*Otogi no Sekai-Ryoku* • *Otogi's World Tour Plus 50,000 Nen* • *More Than 50,000*

*Urikohime to Amanjaku* • *The Little Devil and Princess Uriko*

*Osamu ni Natta Kitsune* • *The Fox Who Became King*

*Beer Mukashi Mukashi* • *Once Upon a Time There Was Beer*

*Chibi Kuro Sambo no Tora Taiji* • *Little Black Sambo Conquers the Tigers*

**VIII: International Explosion: pages 236–241**

*Anju to Zushiomaru/Anju and Zushiomaru* • *The Littlest Warrior*

*Wanpaku Oji no Orochi Taiji* • *The Little Prince and the Eight-Headed Dragon*

*Arabian Night: Sindbad no Boken* • *Sinbad the Sailor*

*Gulliver no Uchu Ryoko* • *Gulliver's Adventures Beyond the Moon*

*Andersen Monogatari* • *The World of Hans Christian Andersen*

*Nagagutsu o Haita Neko* • *Puss in Boots*

*Taiyo no Oji: Hols no Boken* • *The Little Norse Prince, a.k.a. The Sun Prince; Hols' Great Adventure and The Little Norse Prince Valiant*

*Cyborg 009: Kaiju Senso* • *Cyborg 009: Fighting Monsters*

*Soratobu Yureisen* • *The Flying Phantom Ship*

*Kaitei 30,000 Mile* • *30,000 Miles Under the Sea*

*Otogi Manga Calendar* • *Otogi Cartoon Calendar*

*Tetsuwan Atom* • *Astro Boy, a.k.a. Mighty Atom*

*Tetsujin 28-go* • *Gigantor, a.k.a. Iron Man No. 28*

*Eight Man* • *8th Man*

*Takarajima* • *Treasure Island Revisited*

*Jungle Taitei* • *Kimba the White Lion, a.k.a. Jungle Emperor*

*Mahotsukai Sally* • *Sally the Little Witch*

*Ribon no Kishi* • *Princess Knight, a.k.a. Choppy and the Princess*

*Ge Ge Ge no Kitaro* • *Kitaro's (Scary Ghost Moon), a.k.a. Kitaro's Booooo!*

*Sabu to Ichi Torimono Hikae* • *The Detective Stories of Sabu and Ichi*

*Sazae-san* • *Mrs Sazae*

*Ashita no Joe* • *Tomorrow's Joe*

*Tenma no Torayan* • *Torayan on the Boat*

*Ningen Dobutsuen* • *The Human Zoo*

*Isu* • *The Chair*

*Satsujinkyo Jidai* • *The Maniac Age*

*Hana* • *Flower*

*Ookami Shonen Ken* • *Ken the Wolf Boy*

*Tsukiyo to Megane* • *A Moonlit Night and Eyeglasses*

**IX: Animation For Grown-Ups: pages 260–261**

*Lupin III* • *Lupin III: The Mystery of Mamo, a.k.a. Lupin the 3rd: The Secret of Mamo and Lupin vs. the Clones*

*Lupin III: Cagliostro no Shiro* • *The Castle of Cagliostro*

*Mazinger Z* • *Mazinger Z, a.k.a. TranZor Z*

*Kido Senshi Gundam* • *Mobile Suit Gundam*

*Uchu Senkan Yamato* • *Space Cruiser Yamato, a.k.a. Space Battleship Yamato and Star Blazers*

*Ginga Tetsudo 999* • *Galaxy Express 999*

*Kagaku Ninja-Tai Gatchaman* • *Battle of the Planets, a.k.a. G-Force*

*Versailles no Bara* • *The Rose of Versailles*

*Pika-Don* • *a.k.a. Pica-Don*

*Ittai Yatsu wa Nanimonodo?* • *What on Earth Is He?*

*Nihonjin* • *The Japanese*

*Hana Ori* • *Breaking Branches is Forbidden*

*Oni* • *The Devil*

*Tabi* • *The Journey*

*Shijin no Shogai* • *The Life of a Poet*

*Dojoji* • *Dojoji Temple*

*Kataku* • *House of Flames*

*Ame no Hi* • *Imagination*

*Bavel no Hon* • *Bavel's Book*

*Dottini Suru!* • *Your Choice!*

**X: New Directions: pages 294–299**

*Genma Taisen* • *Harmageddon*

*Oneamisu no Tsubasa: Oritsu Uchugun* • *The Wings of Honneamise: Royal Space Force*

*Golgo 13* • *Golgo 13: The Professional*

*Urusei Yatsura* • often translated as *Those Obnoxious Aliens*, but released in the US under the Japanese title

*Maison Ikkoku* • the name of a boarding house, released in the US under the Japanese title

*Ranma 1/2* • sometimes translated as *Ranma Half-and-Half or Halfway Ranma*, but released in the US under the Japanese title

*Dr Slump Arale-chan* • *Dr Slump (and) Little Arale*, unreleased in the US but well-known to anime fans as *Dr Slump*

*Chojiku Yosai Macross* • *Macross, the Super-Dimensional Fortress*, usually known as just *Macross*

*Hokuto no Ken* • *Fist of the North Star*

*Maho no Tenshi Creamy Mami* • *Creamy Mami, the Magical Angel*

*Kido Keisatsu Patlabor* • *Mobile Police Patlabor*

*Yoju Toshi* • *Wicked City*

*Manie Manie Meikyu Monogatari* • *Neo Tokyo*

*Hadashi no Gen* • *Barefoot Gen*

*Hotaru no Haka* • *Grave of the Fireflies*

*Natsufuku no Shojotachi* • *Girls in Summer Dresses*

*Hi no Ame ga Furu* • *Raining Fire*

*Ushiro no Shomen Daaaare* • *Kayoko's Diary*

*Ohoshi-sama no Rail* • *Rail of the Star*

*Kaze no Tani no Nausicaä* • *Nausicaä of the Valley of the Winds*

*Tenku no Shiro: Laputa* • *Laputa: The Castle in the Sky a.k.a. The Castle in the Sky*

*Tonari no Totoro* • *My Neighbor Totoro*

*Majo no Takkyubin* • *Kiki's Delivery Service*

*Omohide Poroporo* • *Only Yesterday*

*Kurenai no Buta* • *Porco Rosso*

*Heisei Tanuki Gassen Pompoko* • *Pom Poko*

*Mononoke Hime* • *Princess Mononoke*

*Sen to Chihiro no Kamikakushi* • *Spirited Away*

*Mimi no Sumaseba* • *Whisper of the Heart*

*Neko no Ongaeshi* • *The Cat Returns*

*Roujin Z* • *Old Man Z*

*Metropolis* • *Metropolis, a.k.a. Osamu Tezuka's Metropolis*

*San Ge Heshang* • *The Three Monks*

*San Mao Liu Lang Ji* • *The Wanderings of San Mao*

*Yu Bang Xiang Zheng* • *The Snipe-Clam Grapple*

**XI: Renaissance: pages 330–331**

*Kido Keisatsu Patlabor* • *Patlabor: The Movie*

*Kido Keisatsu Patlabor 2* • *Patlabor 2*

*Havoc in Heaven, a.k.a. Uproar in Heaven*

*Cao Yuan Ying Xiong Jie Mie* • *Two Heroic Sisters of the Grasslands*

*Mu Di* • *Buffalo Boy and the Flute*

*Kokaku Kidotai* • *Ghost in the Shell*

*Blood: Blood: The Last Vampire*

*Jubei Ninpocho* • *Ninja Scroll*

*Totsuzen! Neko no Kuni Banipal Witt* • *Catnapped!*

*Pocket Monster* • *Pokémon*

*Digimon Adventure* • *Digimon: Digital Monsters*

*Monster Farm* • *Monster Rancher*

*Meitantei Conan* • *Detective Conan a.k.a. Case Closed*

*Bishojo Senshi Sailor Moon* • *Sailor Moon*

*Card Captor Sakura* • *CardCaptors*

*Shojo Kakumei Utena* • *Revolutionary Girl Utena*

*Shinseiki Evangelion* • *Neon Genesis Evangelion*

*Fushigi no Umi no Nadia* • *Nadia: The Secret of Blue Water*

*Lodoss to Senki* • *Record of Lodoss War*

*Ihotov no Kensa: Kenji no Haru* • *Spring and Chaos*

*Tenku no Escaflowne* • *The Vision of Escaflowne*

*Ao no Roku-go* • *Blue Submarine No. 6*

*Fushigina Elevator* • *The Elevator*

*Ouchi* • *A House*

*Sandoitti* • *The Sandwiches*

**XII: The New Century: pages 366–373**

*Cowboy Bebop: Tengoku no Tobira* • *Cowboy Bebop: Knockin' on Heaven's Door a.k.a. Cowboy Bebop: The Movie*

*WXIII: Patlabor the Movie 3 a.k.a. Patlabor WXIII The Movie and Wasted 13 Patlabor the Movie*

*Sennen Joyu* • *Millennium Actress*

*Palme no Ki* • *A Tree of Palme*

*Seikai no Monshou* • *Crest of the Stars*

*Megami Kouhosei* • *Pilot Candidate, a.k.a. Candidate for Goddess*

*Chitcha no Yukitsukai: Sugar* • *Sugar: A Little Snow Fairy*

*Kokaku Kidotai: Stand Alone Complex* • *Ghost in the Shell: Stand Alone Complex*

*Jubei Ninpocho: Ryuhogyoku-hen* • *Ninja Scroll: The Series*

*Chikyu Shoujo Arjuna* • *Arjuna*

*Mousou Dairinin* • *Paranoia Agents*

*Nekojiru-so* • *Cat Soup*

*Hoshi no Koe* • *Voices of a Distant Star*

*Sentou Yousei Yukikaze* • *Yukikaze*

*Atama-yama* • *Mt Head*

*Wo Wei Ge Kuang* • *Music Up*

*Mai Dou Gu Shi (Mandarin)/Mak Dau Goo Si (Cantonese)* • *My Life As McDull*

*Final Fantasy: The Spirits Within, a.k.a. Final Fantasy*